The
Conscious
Creative

The Conscious Creative

Practical
Ethics for
Purposeful
Work

Kelly Small

AMBROSIA

Published in Canada in 2020 and the USA in 2020 by House of Anansi Press Inc.
www.houseofanansi.com

House of Anansi Press is committed to protecting our natural environment. This book is made of material from well-managed FSC®-certified forests, recycled materials, and other controlled sources. The paper is manufactured using renewable energy (Biogas) and processed chlorine-free.

24 23 22 21 20   1 2 3 4 5

Library and Archives Canada Cataloguing in Publication

Title: The conscious creative : practical ethics for purposeful work / Kelly Small.
Names: Small, Kelly, author.
Identifiers: Canadiana (print) 20200198025 | Canadiana (ebook) 20200198033 |
ISBN 9781487008024 (softcover) | ISBN 9781487008031 (EPUB) |
ISBN 9781487008048 (Kindle)
Subjects: LCSH: Cultural industries—Employees—Conduct of life.
Classification: LCC HD9999.C9472 S63 2020 | DDC 174/.97—dc23

Book design: Alysia Shewchuk

We acknowledge for their financial support of our publishing program the Canada Council for the Arts, the Ontario Arts Council, and the Government of Canada.

House of Anansi Press respectfully acknowledges that the land on which we operate is the traditional territory of many Nations, including the Mississaugas of the Credit, the Anishnabeg, the Chippewa, the Haudenosaunee, and the Wendat peoples.

Printed and bound in Canada

For the creatives who never
start a project without asking
if something more meaningful
can be achieved

Contents

Introduction

Let's start by setting an intention.

This book aims to clarify the complicated business of achieving an ethical practice in the creative industries, or, in other words, becoming a more conscious creative.

The humble support in this book will be particularly relevant to those of us who work in the creative economy, which employs over 14 million of us in the United States, approximately 2.5 million in the U.K., and 2.25 million in Canada.[1] Creative skill sets are increasingly employed outside of these traditionally creative industries too. It stands to reason that with so many of us committing our work-lives to producing the sort of cultural content that influences worldviews, impacts purchase decisions, and informs our interactions with the earth and each other that some ethical consideration might be pertinent.

In the spirit of inclusivity and a personal conviction that we're all creative at our core, I offer this book in the hope it will be useful for any of us interested in learning simple methods to be more mindful and intentional about our impact.

The Conscious Creative is written with the belief that when responsible action is made accessible and judgement is withdrawn, we're all a whole lot less scared to put in the work to make positive, incremental changes to our daily work-lives — regardless of where we work or for whom, and despite acts of questionable ethical merit from our pasts. This is a safe space, friends.

Rigid codes of ethical behaviour are not what this book is about. Nor is it a contribution to esoteric philosophical debate. It is, instead, a collection of over 100 ethical choose-what-works-for-you actions from professional experience, rigorous research, and the practices of industry experts whose work includes a daily infusion of moral action and principled thinking. (You can skip ahead to where the actions begin on page 27.)

Where is this coming from?

The Conscious Creative's varying and comprehensive guidance is crafted from ideas borrowed from ethics, activism, sustainability, social justice, and social innovation. It intends to be a unique contribution to an evolving zeitgeist and support toward the realization of our collective ethical potential in an uncertain age of climate crises, pandemics, and social transformation across the political spectrum.

The actions are organized with inspiration from Stuart Walker's Quadruple Bottom Line of Sustainability[2] and ikigai philosophy[3]—both of which are far less complicated than they sound. In each approach, achieving a fulfilling practice capable of standing the test of time means addressing how we support the earth, other people, and our emotional selves, while radically (though perhaps reluctantly) accepting the current reality of our capitalist overlords and pragmatically factoring in how we intend to earn a living.

Most importantly, no matter our prior familiarity with ethical action and regardless of which corner of the industry we find ourselves in, each of us can do something.

Right now.

Welcome to the conscious community (you're awesome for being here)

The Conscious Creative is for anyone in the creative industries who has ever felt like they had to compromise their personal ethics for the sake of their professional practice.

Let's do a quick survey to see how many of the following resonate. I have:

- ▶ Used my skills to sell or support a person, product, or service I morally disagree with

- ▶ Created something without making sure it was accessible to everybody

- ▶ Been witness to or experienced discrimination, stereotyping, or inequitable representation

- ▶ Promoted questionable consumable products

- ▶ Participated in the creation of a habit-forming digital experience

- ▶ Influenced users toward an unintended purchase or behaviour

- ▶ Worked with clients or companies with harmful environmental and/or social practices

- ▶ Shared images, fonts, or intellectual property without giving credit to the copyright holders

- ▶ Contributed to overconsumption

- ▶ Created something using unsustainable materials

- ▶ Overlooked a problematic supply chain

- ▶ Exploited an audience's psychological vulnerabilities to sell a product

For those of us earning in the creative industries (and beyond), many of these ethical transgressions can happen on the daily. If you're anything like my colleagues and me, the too-real jokes about selling our souls to make a living aren't coming out of nowhere.

The term "creative economy" was coined in 2001,[4] but the act of increasing the value of a product or idea through creative imagination has existed much longer. Some historians agree that industries like communication design, advertising, and marketing were born out of a burgeoning need to promote the mass-produced wares of the Industrial Revolution.[5] I would argue that nearly all of the creative industries evolved into their current incarnations from that historical pivot point too. Since the turn of the (previous) century, we've become impressively sophisticated in our approaches to persuasion, and the lines between so-called strategy and manipulation to purchase are increasingly blurred. So, is it true that asking creative folks not to persuade is like asking "fishermen [ahem, *people*] not to fish"?[6] Or can we continue to do the work that we do and also liberate ourselves from our roles in hyper-consumption and the environmental and psychological degradation that often accompany it? Are there small actions we can make immediately to create change in a set of industries historically preoccupied by their misdeeds[7] but reticent to propose anything actionably different?

I believe there are.

Practitioners of the design industry have been particularly outspoken against the implications of consumer culture and have advocated for creativity's potential as a change agent since design's early days as a distinct practice. Fifty years ago, the German Ulm School was founded on the notion that design must contribute to a "socially responsible construction of the world."[8] In Britain in 1964, Ken Garland and thirty other creatives published the *First Things First* manifesto to implore an advertising-saturated society to reconsider its priorities. And in 1971, Papanek's *Design for the Real World* called on American practitioners to create for human needs and not for unsustainable, manufactured wants. The creative industry was dominated by a uniform demographic[9] dissenting but, arguably, doing little to shift responsibilities in a rapidly transforming, increasingly complex world. Over the years, despite numerous calls-to-action and manifestos,[10] those early rallying cries remained largely unheeded in many sectors of the industry.

Fast-forward to now. We creatives continue to voice our discontentment in industries whose incredible potential is so often bound by the bottom line. Innumerable tweets, articles, and posts engage in call-out culture, where we publicly shame unethical leaders and companies. Big-tech workers participate in global walkouts to protest climate inaction, working conditions, and corporate connections to human rights abuses. We talk a lot about the environmental threat of fast fashion, the emotional and physical damage that can result from toxic aspects of the beauty industry, and the psychological perils of an unregulated ten-billion-dollar influencer marketing industry.

Creatives care and we always have. We may not have all the answers to the ethical questions that plague us. We may often feel overwhelmed by the scale of the problems we face. We may not always have access to the most effective methods of enacting positive change but, relentlessly, we try.

Our subservience to an arguably problematic **capitalist system**[11] hasn't stopped us from identifying areas for improvement and challenging the status quo.

> **What's so bad about capitalism, the lite version: issues of rising wealth inequality, the prevalence of money from special interest groups influencing increasingly polarized politics, a fast-growing financial sector making economic theories based on production irrelevant, deregulation resulting in "necessary" compromises (to things like human rights, safety, and environmental impact) in the name of the bottom line, and an unsustainable growth model.[12]**

There are a number of emerging and extremely promising areas of creative practice that are founded on the pursuit of a more sustainable and equitable world. We'll cover them. In the coming pages, we'll learn to activate our practices to subvert from within profit-focused structures to become ethically minded and action-oriented change makers.

But first, let me introduce myself.

Capitalism: ~~A Love Story~~ It's Complicated

I grew up at the mall. I was born into a family whose livelihood relied on the exploding consumer culture of the '80s and '90s. My father ran shopping centres. My mom managed finances for several of the stores within. Brands are kind of in my blood.

As a kid, I played hide-and-seek in the labyrinth of corridors and indulged my family in chubby-smiled modelling (term used loosely) in back-to-school fashion shows and a local Sears catalogue. In my adolescence I was auditioning identities in change rooms and privileged enough to buy mood rings and a coveted Guess jean jacket. I bought *Seventeen* magazine every month and its ads guided awkward attempts at attracting my classmates by wearing particular brands, instilled a perceived need to own every angsty album that was released, and solidified an appreciation for Doc Martens that remains rather persistent. And at my first job? I learned to lubricate the purchase of overpriced sport sunglasses to the considerable number of performance athletes in small-town Ontario—no shock, at the mall.

Design was a fitting career choice. Like me at the time, its value and identity relied largely upon its proximity to the popular brands of the day. It's entirely unsurprising that I landed in advertising while completing my first design degree at OCAD University. With my intimate understanding of the creation of desire, it's even less surprising that I stuck it out until my mid-thirties. I rose to the role of creative director quickly, and before I knew it, I had won some awards and was developing strategies to sell some of the biggest brands in the world.

What was surprising, however, was that throughout all of this I often had a copy of *Adbusters* magazine on my bedside table. There was a latent skepticism just below the surface of my heavily branded lifestyle and career. It was subconsciously urging me toward a new ethics and awareness about the threats posed by the ever-more-sophisticated, hyper-targeted world of marketing and rampant consumerism that I was contributing to, rather passionately, every day of my life.

As one might expect, the dormant doubts inevitably surfaced. My health suffered as I struggled to find purpose while feeling trapped in the clutches of a consumption machine. My once-impassioned approach to creative briefs that sought solutions for sophisticated persuasions became a painful slog. I was using the power of design to strategically manipulate millions of target consumers (people, citizens) to use toxic products, eat food devoid of nutritional value, beautify their appearances (implying they were less-than-adequate before), and "upgrade" their technology and vehicles needlessly. I also witnessed rampant stereotyping, discrimination, shocking homogeneity, and a deep gender divide—I was one of **only 3 percent** of creative directors at the time who weren't cis men.[13] That number drops significantly if we additionally factor in racialized identities, gender variance, and intersections like queer communities of colour.

> **The 3% Movement** was started in 2013 to address an abysmally low statistic that showed 3 percent of creative directors to be female.* That number has since risen to approximately 11 percent at the time of writing. **3percentmovement.com**
>
> *Gender variance outside the binary was not accounted for in this study. Maybe next time.

I had become critically conscious of the extent to which my industry and practice were not contributing to the betterment of society and, suddenly, it was all I could see.

My existential career crisis continued to escalate, but on paper I had a great job in a global digital firm. My clients at the time included the world's most profitable toy company, one of Canada's "Big 3" telecom companies, and a major automotive brand. Gratefully, I also worked on a lone non-profit client, the gender-equity brand of one of the country's largest charities. For years I had done my best to ensure I was always working with at least one non-profit client. This one, like those before it, provided a soft(ish) place to land for my sullied ad-industry soul. It was a welcome break from a world where bright minds make big money to invent the needs that sustain the beast of unbridled consumerism. As imperfect as the non-profit industry can be, it offered an opportunity to think beyond single-minded financial return and design meaningful work that could support positive change.

It also affirmed my discontentment with the way things were.

So I quit my job and sold and donated almost everything I owned. I set off to figure out a way to put ethics at the forefront of my creative practice. I was certain, at that time, that ethics and capitalism could not coexist. I was prepared (albeit terrified) to reject everything I had done in my career to date and find a new way forward.

I was fortunate enough to pursue my master's degree at Emily Carr University, where I learned to use design research techniques to explore responsible creative practice. I would be lying (inadvisable in a book about ethics) if I implied that this transition was easy. Dismantling a lifetime of material-ism and an identity where I had unconsciously decided that my value was directly correlated to my earning potential was incredibly complicated.

Further, my research was leading nowhere viable. I discovered many academics who espoused the tenets of a utopian creative sector freed from capitalist ideals, but whose writings offered not a single method about how to make rent as an ethically minded creative person. I felt stuck. Not shockingly, I got depressed. Like, real-deal mental health crisis still-on-meds depressed. But that's a story unto itself. One day when the darkness was lifting, I stumbled across a visualization of ikigai philosophy that posed the following questions:

What do you love?
What are you good at?
What does the world need?

And this was the kicker for me:

What can you be paid for?

I loved this diagram. It was the inspiration I needed to get unstuck. I realized that all of these things can coexist... and, more realistically, that all this *must* coexist. Human goodness and the desire to improve the world is as real as the capitalist paradigm in which we work. I can't singlehandedly overthrow the dominant economic system, but what I can do is subvert the system from within to realize meaningful change. I started asking myself, how can I earn money doing what I love in service (mostly, but not exclusively) to what the world needs?

This is the sweet spot for the conscious creative. Philosophy often feels idealistic and impossible to realize in real-life practice. Conversely, commerce can feel soul-sucking and inhuman. An achievable, balanced ethical practice doesn't *require* a total lifestyle overhaul.

Given the right opportunities, most people want to do better. For those, like me, who are committed to earning a living being creative in the most ethical way possible, the clear, non-judgemental, ethically driven guidance in this book can help to do exactly that.

So, let's get started.

Easy ethics for creative types

No pressure, but we're operating in largely unregulated industries. That means the responsibility for ethical action is up to each of us. Doctors have the Hippocratic Oath; psychologists have to register with their licensing body that governs ethical practice; accountants and financial analysts are bound by the ethical standards of their various certifications. Creatives? Creatives have inspirational tweets by industry demigods and a collection of impassioned manifestos. Not as helpful.

Ethics in the creative industries—and ethics in general—can be extremely subjective. It is the conscience of each of us, the practitioners, that determines the moral framework that guides our decisions.[14] So, for better or for worse, it is important for each of us to educate ourselves on the topic of ethics and morality.

Cue the crash course.

Morality is concerned with the principles of right and wrong behaviour, and the goodness or badness of human character. Ethics is the branch of philosophy dealing with that morality.

The term "ethical" has a few definitions. First: *relating to the discipline dealing with what is good and bad or with moral duty and obligation.*[15] Second: *morally good and correct.* Third: *to avoid activities or organizations that do harm to people, animals, and the environment.*[16]

So, for our purposes here, ethical practice is the act of creating with the intent to be morally good and avoid social and ecological harm. Unethical practice is its mindless or ill-intending counterpart. These are the basic definitions on which this book is predicated.

I often think about an article in a popular industry magazine that carried an ironic but memorable title: "Design Is Inherently an Unethical Industry."[17] It featured reader-led discussions about morality and virtue in the industry with a special focus on product design and tech. In it, a handful of contributors offer arguments that the creative industry can never be considered "good" as long as we prioritize client and financial interests over the needs of our users and audience.

Written with little nuance and, of course, sensationalized for those delicious clicks, the article positioned money-earning and money-making creative work as essentially amoral. It left little room for us regular rent-paying types to do our jobs without feeling like we are completely selling our souls.

It evokes the work of theorist Tony Fry, who writes that if a creative industry is to achieve ethical status, it must separate from a market economy that values the production of sweet, sweet wealth (my language) over improving people's lives.[18] I certainly can't argue with the logic. I can, however, fall down a rabbit hole of debilitating existential crises (again) at having no idea how to continue existing in the modern world while living in an anti-capitalist commune. But I digress.

Other contributors to the "Unethical" article argue that we creative folks are just humans wielding tools that can be used for good or for evil, regardless of how complicit we are in capitalist endeavours. Practically speaking, this resonates with me a lot more than a theoretical pursuit of extricating all creative work from the marketplace. In the article, one user shares a poignant example—that for all of the horrifying privacy violations and fake news Facebook helped to spread, it also facilitated crucial communication during the Arab Spring and has connected people in ways that were formerly impossible. This is an essential reminder for conscious creative thinkers that bringing something new into existence invariably results in a spectrum of unintended consequences.[19]

At the turn of the twenty-first century, media theorist and de facto tech prophet **Neil Postman** declared that our relationship with emerging technology was something of a Faustian bargain. He said, "Technology giveth and technology taketh away."[20]

His point?

For every advantage a new technology offers, there are often a host of unconsidered societal effects: some positive, some not so positive. So, the way I see it, in order to be ethical creators, it is vital that we start by considering the social, cultural, political, and economic impacts of our creations—knowing that *creative practice* giveth and *creative practice* taketh away. It's up to each of us, in every decision we make, to mindfully do our best to avoid creating those not-so-positive effects.

> **Neil Postman** died in 2003, sadly, missing the advent of social media and what was an impressive and arguably unequivocal confirmation of his philosophies about emerging technology.
>
> Check out his prophetic "Five Things We Need to Know about Technological Change."

Where this leaves me on the topic of creativity and ethics is with a steadfast belief that the notion of an inherently unethical industry with absolute ideals about goodness and badness simply does not exist. In a famous analogy, French philosopher Bruno Latour reminds us that it wasn't until Frankenstein neglected and abandoned his monster that it became truly monstrous.[21] If we follow Latour's wisdom, later expanded on by **María Puig de la Bellacasa**, by compassionately tending to and nurturing our creations to mitigate their potentially harmful effects, then we're well on our way to a more ethical practice. Further, if cultivating a more conscious, nurturing practice is essential to responsible work, then ethical work is a lot like the care we provide our loved ones—it is an organic, reciprocal, ongoing practice and not a rigid set of rules to be adhered to. Nodding? Me too. This supports my research that found industry practitioners to be pretty ambivalent about rigid, traditional codes of ethics.

> **Consider reading de la Bellacasa's *Matters of Care* for an in-depth exploration of the ethics and politics of care through a feminist science and technology studies lens.**

Collectively, the creative industries have somewhere around sixty codes of ethics but none of those, outside of those necessary for architectural licensing, are regulated or compulsory.

As a result, we creatives have hundreds—maybe thousands—of optional rules to follow, but most of us have no governing body that mandates a specified level of ethical education. No studying. No exams. No mandatory certifications prior to starting our practice.[22] There is no official Hippocratic Oath for creatives, although attempts have been made.[23] Formal creative education excels in developing critical thinkers, but it often fails to address the practical ethical issues that arise in working life. In the absence of comprehensive **codes of conduct**, we must actively choose to make ethical practice a part of our careers and commit to the ongoing task of developing our own sets of ethical parameters.

Jump to creative industry codes of ethics in the Resources section on page 193.

I interviewed and surveyed a cross-section of over 130 people in the creative industries, including folks from tech, design, communications, marketing, and advertising. Only five of those people referenced an industry code of ethics.

Not one person cited a specific rule.

I can't say I'm surprised. I have spent over fifteen years in professional creative life and not once did an employer, an educator, or colleague make reference to a code of ethics.

Is it that we don't care? Or could it be that these inflexible methods of imparting ethical guidance aren't particularly accessible nor are they designed to vibe with the fluidity and multifariousness of our everyday working lives?

I choose to believe the latter, and my research supports this. In her book *Good*, creative Lucienne Roberts interviews philosopher Anthony Grayling, who confidently shares that an ethical code of conduct is too awkward and inflexible for complex and deeply subjective creative professions. Their conversation suggests that creative folks may do better with a focus on actionable examples of responsible practice to support them in making ethical choices at the individual level.[24] I'm partial to this suggestion, because the actions in this book aim to do exactly that.

Aristotle believed that moral behaviour is something we can get better at. According to him, an ethical life manifests through the actions we take and, lucky for us, the more we practice, the more we improve.[25]

Challenges (Wait, you said this was easy...)

You know what? I take issue with the suggestion that the most important ethical decision we creatives can make is whether to accept a job.[26]

As we've all witnessed in the aggressive social dynamics of **cancel or call-out culture**, boycotts can be powerful— particularly in the case of consumer activism, where mass moral outrage stands to tarnish an offender's reputation[27] or temporarily compromise economic stability. But in the case of walking away from a client or creative project on ethical grounds, don't we risk passing the job on to someone less likely to challenge its morally questionable issues? Don't we relinquish an opportunity to understand the nuances of the problem, have influence, or make change from the inside?[28]

> **Cancel culture** is a social media phenomenon describing a mass boycott usually directed at a single person who is "cancelled" by fans or followers due to actions or opinions believed to be unjust. Cancel culture can be empowering and voice-giving for marginalized folks advocating for social justice and is argued to become problematic when accusations are without merit or the accused is not given space to learn from their mistakes.

Undoubtedly, there will be times when a project or client is so morally deplorable that declining the brief and speaking out is the best way forward. Making that decision is up to each of us in the moment. The average project decision, however, is often far less cut-and-dried.

It's important not to fall into the reductive view that anything in the arts, non-profit, or public sector is ethically A-okay and anything corporate is fundamentally corrupt. Public and private sector organizations can be deeply interrelated through tax funding and corporate sponsorship, for example. It's also hard to discern how "clean" an individual charitable donation really is.

The lesson?

We must do our research.

It's important that we acknowledge the complexity of the issues involved when questioning the ethical merit of any project or organization. Often, it's less about the type of business or organization and more about its practices.

Ethics in creative industries can be broken down by legalities, integrity, and morality. [29] The first two are well-explored areas as they relate to professional practice. They're the common-place issues like **licensing, piracy, plagiarism and appropriation, spec work**, deceptive practices, and the basics of being a stand-up professional who takes seriously their responsibilities to clients, audiences, and fellow creatives. The industry is saturated with resources on legalities and professional integrity and this book will cover some of the more pressing issues. But if I'm honest—which, again, I should try to be—my interest lies more in the category of morality and the actions we can take to start addressing our complicity in the larger social and ecological consequences of our industries.

Licensing: Payment for the use of creative resources, fonts, images

Piracy: Unauthorized use or reproduction of work, often programs, fonts, etc.

Plagiarism and appropriation: Passing off someone else's work as one's own

Spec work: Providing creative work without an agreed-upon fee or contract

As creatives responsible for mass communication and millions of audience impressions per minute, we've got a lot of power to make an impact. For better or worse, we creative types deeply affect the way information is interpreted, how brands and products are consumed,[30] and the ways that people experience the mediated and artificial world.[31] We're behind content creation and big-brand marketing messages, repackaging reality through storytelling, engineering the experiences of billion-plus-user social media and gaming platforms, designing the way people connect in public spaces, and producing those bewilderingly relevant ads that some-how know what we want before we've even said it out loud.

Given this power, conscious creatives have a responsibility to stay connected to the most pressing issues that society faces—things like gender equity movements (including Time's Up,[32] #MeToo,[33] and **depatriarchisation**[34]), matters of ableism and ageism, trans and queer visibility, rights, and inclusion, racial justice and **decolonization**,[35] hyper-consumption and sustainable practices, and the growing list of issues around online privacy, data, addictive experience design, and deceptive technology, to name a few.

To **depatriarchise** is to examine and address the complicity of creative industries in perpetuating cis male-dominated oppressive systems.

Decolonization refers to the ongoing economic, political, and theoretical processes of healing and reframing narratives relating to the effects of colonial oppression, genocide, and cultural assimilation.

There have been major strides toward a more ethical creative sector in the past few years. The list is long, but here's a start. Canada's leading the charge with its sector-wide mouthful of a movement, the Canadian Creative Industries Code of Conduct to Prevent and Respond to Harassment, Discrimination, Bullying and Violence.[36] We've got the 50/50 Initiative[37] and the 3% Movement[38] addressing gender equity. An impressive number of social good and sustainability awards[39] and even advertising's "Oscars," Cannes Lions, is jumping on board to award brands who dedicate their spending to address global issues.[40] Last year's AIGA Design Census shows us that ethics remains among the most important issues to creative industry practitioners.[41] We have numerous conferences like the Media Ethics conference, FITC, Architect@Work, All Tech Is Human, AnxietyTech, Design Thinkers, and SXSW Design with core content dedicated to creative responsibility.[42] Architecture, media, art, and design schools are shifting away from abstract and commercial assignments to projects with a more critical social and environmental lens.[43] We're beginning to address the problem of discrimination and homogeneity in our industries with more awareness, inclusion, and cultural support for folks from all sorts of backgrounds—across race, gender, ability, sexuality, and beyond. Gratefully, more enlightened approaches to hiring, collaboration, research, and organizational diversity and inclusion are quickly become requisite.[44] There is, of course, significant work to be done. Programs like the Black Youth Design Initiative in Toronto, UNESCO's You Are Next: Empowering Creative Women, the A11Y project for web accessibility, the Queer Design Club (international), and the New York–based ADCOLOR Awards, which honour creative professionals of colour, are all helping to make progress.

Beyond all of this movement, there are emerging areas of practice such as the shift toward humane technology,[45] social innovation toward sustainability,[46] the development of social impact design, and various creative movements with advocacy at their core. These areas share a mission to rethink the practitioner's role in society as less a tool of capitalism and more a support for the betterment of the world we live in. Undeniably, we're witnessing a shift toward a more equitable and impact-aware set of creative industries.

Regardless of where we are individually on our journeys toward conscious creative practice, each of us can take comfort in the fact that we're joining a growing mass of ethically minded practitioners with a passion and willingness to share resources and advice. The insatiable bottom line persists in driving business decisions that stand to compromise life's ability to thrive on this planet. That's just a fact. However, change is happening. Every new participant in the conscious creative movement brings us a step closer to realizing our collective goals.

Worthy challenges, right?

Jumping into action

I've always loved manifestos: Compact packets of concentrated inspiration dripping in idealism and dreamy declarations of possibility. Inspirational and encouraging as manifestos are, they also tend to conclude before giving readers any practical steps to realize the messages they espouse. While providing an outline of the "how" may not be a manifesto's job, its absence can mean that even the most widely shared texts lose momentum before their values are implemented.

What I believe we require now are simple, accessible, and, most importantly, actionable resources to support us in actually living our values in our everyday careers. "Vision without execution, after all, is just a hallucination"—according to Edison or Einstein or an ancient Japanese proverb,[47] anyway. We could also say that taking ethical action is a lot like one of my favourite definitions of creative practice: "the application of intent."[48] Many of us experience a desire to integrate our inner values and our careers—the desire part is easy—but we often struggle to apply that intention in any sort of practical way. Actionable and realistic ethical guidance is crucial if we are to translate our most optimistic ideals into the sort of behaviour that can satisfy our moral selves without compromising our ability to buy lunch (or pay rent, or order the fancy cat litter—whatever you're into).

In my research, I delved into everything from manifestos to industry publications to countless blogs, articles, social posts, and academic papers, exploring popular and academic publishing in the areas of responsible practice, creative citizenship, and practical ethics. I also talked to a wide range of creative professionals. The result is a comprehensive collection of every relevant ethical action I could find. Each is distilled and refined into a succinct parcel of wisdom designed to be easily implemented and support incremental change.

This is creative consciousness in action. This is how to integrate practical ethics into our work. One action step at a time.

Real talk: Ethical practice takes effort. I urge each of us to acknowledge and be proud of the moments when we engage in responsible action toward positive change. But how do we keep it up? How do we establish an ongoing, long-term ethical work-life? Let's turn to the four factors we must consider when building sustainability into our creative practice: **personal, economic, social,** and **environmental**.

Personal is about deciding what matters to us and establishing a strong set of inner values. It means creating a personal climate that fulfills who we are at our core, enables healthy self-care practices, and benefits our inner (spiritual, if that suits) lives. Without first determining what matters to us and establishing a practice that benefits our personal lives and values, we will have no foundation for developing a long-term, sustainable ethical practice.

Economic is about the necessity of earning a living and supporting a professional life where financial success can occur without significantly compromising our values. It means functioning within (though I certainly support critique and action toward change of) our problematic economic system and making the moderate compromises that may be necessary to financially support ourselves and our families within that system. It is a truth for many of us that without that security, our abilities to positively impact each other and the earth are compromised.

Social is about the actions that support positive change for pressing social challenges and our ability to maintain integrity as it relates to establishing equitable practices that benefit communities in need with a foundation of dignity and respect. Social considers how our work impacts each other and how a long-term, sustainable practice is not possible without an effective, healthy social life that includes our local and global communities. Social encourages challenging biases, participatory action, and community involvement.

Environmental is just as it sounds: Action that supports the planet and its creatures. It means operating from a basic understanding that all life on earth has value and that nature itself has rights. By considering climate action and maintaining integrity in our work as it relates to our environment, we protect life and help to sustain a functioning planet—because without it, what do we have? Environmental considers intersectionality and acknowledges that social justice and climate justice are complex and deeply interconnected issues.

By engaging in one or many actions from each of these four factors, we increase our likelihood of achieving a holistic ethical practice that is viable in the long term. Regardless of industry sector or the type of work that we do, many of the actions can be carried out immediately. They're organized to be easily adapted to everyday working life and are listed loosely from the simplest and most accessible to the most challenging.

I truly believe that every single one of us has a creamy creative centre as intrinsic to our humanity as our natural-born moral compasses. It is my hope that these actions will inspire us to tap into that sweet core and enact change, and also to collaborate and support each other as we embark on our journeys as conscious creatives. And remember, conscious action doesn't happen in a vacuum. By modelling the responsible behaviour we want to see in the world, we're naturally motivating our clients, colleagues, suppliers, and families to do the same. I trust that, in time, our collective action will contribute to a critical mass that will make ethical practice a non-negotiable imperative for every creative career.

Now, let's act.

"Actionable ethical guidance is crucial if we are to translate our most optimistic ideals into the sort of behaviour that can satisfy our moral selves without compromising our ability to buy lunch."

Chapter One
Personal Actions

Soul search

Some creative folks believe the most significant decision they can make is to accept a client or project.[1] While it's important not to decline every job with minor infractions as a knee-jerk response, doing some soul-searching and research at the outset of a potential project will help us understand what we could become complicit in by contributing to it. That research may include an assessment of a client's manufacturing processes and supply chains, the safety of their products, and the responsibility of their marketing messages. We may also choose to investigate how sustainably they operate, how inclusive they are, how they manage data and privacy...the list goes on. If we discover that an organization is engaging in less-than-responsible behaviour, it's up to us to decide if a hard decline is the best way forward. Sometimes the best action to take is accepting the brief and intentionally working from inside the organization to make the change we wish to see.

Get to know the global issues

Let's determine what matters most to us. This means famil-iarizing ourselves with the "why" behind our progressive practices and the big systemic issues being faced across the world. The United Nations' Sustainable Development Goals, or SDGs, are the world's plan to establish peace and pros-perity for all people and the planet.[2] These goals include eradicating hunger, poverty, and unemployment; creating equal access to quality education and health care; establish-ing gender equality; and mitigating climate change by putting an end to the degradation of our environment. Countries implement the SDGs with varying focus. Canada, for exam-ple, is committed to implementing the SDGs in a way that prioritizes its most vulnerable and marginalized citizens.[3] This looks like showing sensitivity and paying respectful attention to the unique needs of Indigenous Peoples, people with disabilities, those who identify as LGBTQ2IA+, refugee and immigrant populations, and women and girls.

Commit to self-care

Counter to the utilitarian argument that positions ethics as "the greatest benefit for the greatest number of people," some of us believe that in order to achieve a sustainable "good" in the world, it is imperative to first be good to ourselves.[4] Consider that without sustaining our mental, emotional, and physical health, it's far more challenging to continue our (sometimes) uphill climb toward a viable ethical practice. Further, wading into the treacherous waters of social issues and environmental degradation can be emotionally harrowing. So, let's get into some consistent self-care to support a long and healthy career of putting in the work to stay true to our values. I'm in the bath eating chocolate already. (Listen, some of you are going to be upset with me for minimizing self-care to superficial relaxation. It's more than that. I'm a **spoonie** too, so know the value of deliberate, self-initiated activities that protect our mental, emotional, and physical health. But also chocolate.)

> "Spoonie" is a term for people who live with chronic illness. Spoon theory is a disability metaphor coined by Christine Miserandino in a 2003 essay.[5] A limited number of "spoons" are used to express the reduced amount of energy (physical and mental) available to carry out necessary life tasks due to disability or chronic illness. Check out your local spoon share group for more info or support.

Listen first

Stop. Breathe. Best to quiet the unrelenting voice of the creative mind that urges, "Change something!" or "Make something!" The conscious creative takes the time to listen. Listening is, arguably, the most crucial part of the creative process. Without it, we can miss out on identifying vital connections or understanding the needs, goals, and aspirations of the people we're creating for and with.

Establish an ethical lexicon

The language we use has impacts on our ability to understand the complex issues we're dealing with. Language shapes ideas, influences our capacity to empathize, and contributes to our ability to be informed, respectful, and engaged citizens. Equipping ourselves with the appropriate language to discuss the damaging effects of our industry and support those most affected aids our pursuit of becoming more effective, empathetic allies.

This book contains a glossary of terms (page 205) related to the social, political, economic, and environmental facets of ethical work.

Be mindful of privilege

Most of us are carrying around some sort of privilege. **Privilege** arises from society's tendency to value certain things over others.[6] It means that some of us get advantages in life that others don't and, in many cases, we're unaware of the ways in which our privileges afford us these advantages. Whether it's our gender, ability, race, education, class, religion, sexuality, or neuronormativity, it's important to acknowledge the ways in which our social status has offered us a helping hand.

> **Privilege**, according to the *Oxford English Dictionary*, is "a special right, advantage, or immunity granted or available only to a particular person or group." It is rooted in intersectionality, defined as "the interconnected nature of social categorizations such as race, class, and gender as they apply to a given individual or group, regarded as creating overlapping and interdependent systems of discrimination or disadvantage."

Mindfulness of our privilege(s) is a first step in addressing the wildly disparate systemic advantages and disadvantages faced by various communities. An understanding of privilege supports us as we rethink imbalanced systems in order to create a more equitable world—without it, the development of compassionate and sensitive relationships that make inclusive work possible becomes complicated and fraught. As conscious creatives, being mindful of our privilege means creating with the knowledge that a community's plight can only be known by *that* community. It means respecting the challenges and experiences that shape a community's or an individual's unique worldview and their positions on issues. When collaborating in spaces where disparities in privilege exist, follow some basic best practices: Stay mindful of power dynamics and work to balance them, be compassionate and aware of personal fragility, and share the stories or experiences of collaborators only if explicit consent has been received. Another way to build considerate awareness of other communities is to engage in **media tourism**. We can build empathy by breaking out of our own echo chambers to deliberately learn about the beliefs, issues, and ideas of communities we are not typically connected to.[7]

> **Media tourism** is the act of consciously leaving our hyper-curated, belief-reinforcing online world to check out areas of discourse we would not normally be exposed to. We can follow folks whose politics differ from our own; intentionally click on, like, or follow things we normally wouldn't in order to mess with the algorithms; and adjust newsfeed preferences to show content from sources we sometimes disagree with.

Acknowledge the privilege of ethical practice

Let's make a commitment to avoid judging the people around us whose choices we don't perceive to be the picture of moral responsibility. The ability to make socially and environmentally conscious decisions can be steeped in a privilege not universally shared. For example, ethically made materials, resources, food, and fashion often come at a higher price point and are therefore inaccessible to many people. To have the choice to work for an ethical employer often demands a college education, which requires financial means and a particular learning style. Advocating for change can require long hours, emotional labour, mental fortitude, and a requirement for presence in collective action not always available to those whose safety, mental health, or physical health may be compromised. To be supportive allies in the pursuit of a better world, we must start with an understanding of the complex systems that impact our abilities to act. When we withdraw judgement of other people's choices, we can remember to do the same for ourselves. Usually we are doing the best we can with the awareness and the resources we have at the time.

Challenge your biases

Creating supportive, ethical work environments and experiences means staying conscious of our subtle, unintentional biases. These biases often show themselves as a preference toward likeness or sameness, so best to challenge ourselves to ask questions such as: Why did we chose to create for a specific demographic? Why are we requesting feedback from one colleague and not the other? Why do we want to hire or promote a specific candidate and not another? Why do we invite certain people out for drinks or sit beside them at lunch?[8] Challenging our biases can help to create safer emotional spaces by maximizing inclusion of all ethnicities, genders, sexualities, bodies, and abilities. What's more, when teams better reflect the needs and composition of our audiences, the work has been *proven* more likely to take on a socially responsible dimension. And bonus: We'll model inclusive practices and foster a sense of belonging wherever we work.

Brief with bigger objectives

It's common for creative practitioners to get briefed; that is, to receive an outline of the requirements, objectives, and aspirations for an impending project. How do we get folks to use our stuff? Buy our stuff? Look at our stuff? Love our stuff? Without careful attention, a creative brief can become a single-minded wish list of bottom-line-driven performance indicators where the needs of audiences and the public largely get ignored. Client objectives and the need to turn a profit aren't going anywhere, but we *can* start rewriting our briefs to add an ethical dimension. We may advocate for an additional section of consideration on each creative brief we're involved in by asking, "Who or what does this project help?" Including an adaptation of this question ensures that we never start a project without considering how something bigger than our clients' financial ambitions may be achieved. If the answer to the question is "no one and nothing," which it may often be, then it's up to us and our teams to change that. Let's challenge ourselves to add a new layer of proactive intentions each time we begin a project.

Understand power and create equity

As ethical practitioners, it is crucial we stay on top of emerging conversations that are rooted in social justice. We can educate ourselves on **intersectional feminism** and the ways in which historically oppressed groups—racialized communities, women, girls, trans and gender nonconforming folks—remain marginal in most creative professions and are left fighting for voice, representation, equitable pay, and leadership roles, among other things.[9]

> **The term intersectionality was coined by Kimberlé Crenshaw in 1989 to support an explanation of the oppression of African American women. The term is now central to conversations about racial justice, policing, and identity politics.**

We must do our own personal work as well as contribute to changing practices and policies within wider systems. If nothing else, we need to develop skills and opportunities to have the brave conversations across race, gender, ability, and sexual identities so organizational norms and culture can be expanded to include everyone.

We might look to the design justice network,[10] an approach applicable to all creative fields, that challenges the matrices of domination like white supremacy, cisheteropatriarchy, capitalism, ableism, and settler colonialism and aims to provide an equal distribution of the benefits of creative practice. We can familiarize ourselves with the movement to decolonize creative practice, which acknowledges how societal discourse has been almost exclusively dominated by Anglocentric/Eurocentric ways of "seeing, knowing, and acting in the world, with little attention being paid to the alternative and marginalized discourses from the non-Anglo-European sphere."[11] The integration of non-Anglo-European knowledge, like the work being done to Indigenize curriculums in Canada, is an essential step the creative community can take toward decoloniality. Many institutions around the globe are working to decentralize Western knowledge. There is work to be done. It is up to those of us whose cultures have not suffered the effects of colonialism to inform ourselves; we can examine our beliefs, biases, and relationships in order to begin to dismantle deeply socialized colonial views of the world. Jump to page 204 for resources to learn more.

Practice ethics every day

Like mastering our craft or learning to meditate, ethics are a practice, and the best results come from repetition. In the way that getting swole (as the kids say) or mastering a yogic headstand won't come from a single session, ethical action isn't (ideally) a one-time thing; it requires patience and a consistent commitment over time. The good news? Daily practices don't have to be perfect—we just have to show up and act. Over the course of a career, our cumulative effort can have a ton of impact.

Keep it legal

Hot tip: Don't break the law when it comes to the basics of ethical creative work. Transgressions to avoid include plagiarizing other people's work, neglecting to properly credit collaborators or other authors and makers, not paying for creative resources such as images or fonts, and using resources and tools without the appropriate rights.

Easy, right? Most of us are already nailing the legalities of creative work.

Read your codes of ethics

As we covered in the Introduction, most creatives aren't
fans of rigid codes of ethics—and, full disclosure, neither
am I. That doesn't mean those codes, thrilling as they are,
aren't teeming with important and relevant foundational
information for developing a responsible practice. Consider
using the codes as a starting point but not as the *entire* ethical
foundation of your practice. In fact, many of the codes are in
dire need of an update. Jump to page 193 for a select list of
industry codes of ethics in the Resources section.

Challenge the integrity of your content

As collaborators and vendors, we creatives are often bound to the creations of others—website copy, social media video content, a manuscript, furniture and building supplies, various types of entertainment…the list is long. Each item comes with its own political, social, environmental, and financial implications, and some of those, some of the time, may be problematic. The content we are supplied with is, arguably, never neutral or value-free. It has been said that a piece of creative "has no more integrity than its purpose or subject matter. Garbage in, garbage out."[12]

So, in the same way that it's a publisher's duty to vet the content of their authors' books, it is imperative that all creatives challenge the quality and substance of the content we're provided by clients and colleagues. By doing so, we ensure the project doesn't commit offences like perpetuating harmful stereotypes, supporting unsustainable practices, or manipulating users with false claims. And what if we're provided with content that offends? If it's safe to do so, speak up and advocate for better.

Be a citizen first

We are citizens first and conscious creatives second, so a balanced ethical practice requires considering more than just how and what we make. If we dare to look at the impact of our everyday lifestyle choices, we can bravely ask ourselves how we might do better by people, by animals, and by the planet.

We could begin to shop locally and take transit or cycle. We could consume fewer animal products or, if we do choose to consume them, support free-range farming and humane treatment standards, and seek out products with a commitment to ethical production. We might stop using single-use cups and plastic lids, cutlery, and straws, or even get ourselves some reusable gear. We could trade, mend, and swap pre-loved clothing instead of always buying new garments so we're not supporting the unsustainable fast-fashion industry.[13] Consider, as well, that storing less data means that our carbon footprint lessens significantly, since data farms cause up to 2% of all greenhouse gas emissions.[14] That's as much as air travel, one of the most carbon-intensive aspects of many people's lifestyles. Perhaps the most important question of all is simply: How can we *consume* less and *experience* more?[15]

Ask: What if everybody did that?

One simple question is fundamental to ethical work: "What if everybody did that?" Imagine a world where everybody created in ways that cultivated empowerment. What if everybody adhered to the standard of hiring only while being mindful of unconscious biases? What if every creative person rejected the idea of exploiting psychological vulnerabilities to sell stuff? The same is true for the reverse. If we're leaning toward a decision of questionable ethical merit, imagine the effects of that decision en masse. Decision making is simplified when framed in this way. Let's advocate within our organizations for folks to ask themselves this one little question. It quickly adds a layer of ethical responsibility to those otherwise mundane work-life decisions.

Give every job an ethical orientation

Every job can be an ethical opportunity. If we're committed enough, an otherwise soul-crushing client request can be subverted to cleverly infuse a greater purpose. We may serve our clients well and also think beyond their revenue needs to examine the impact of our creation on our audience, the public, and the earth.

Consider that we might advocate for improved accessibility, make sure all team members are treated fairly, use transparent and honest language, ensure the creative execution is environmentally friendly, work to remove misleading or inflated claims, or even suggest a partnership program where a percentage of proceeds go to a worthy cause. With practice, each of us can develop go-to strategies that help balance the objectives of any project so that the output succeeds on multiple levels.

Add ethics to your ethos

Many creatives have a philosophy or ethos that they share through portfolio sites, social channels, industry publications, resumés, and even email signatures. If our work has even the slightest ethical dimension, let's not be afraid to publicize that area of our pursuits. By doing so, we will generate necessary awareness about the conscious creative movement and keep ourselves accountable to our greater career goals. Think you don't have a philosophy? Not sure how to describe it? Most of us follow principles or beliefs, though often we haven't had to be specific about them. A good place to start is by adopting aspects of the philosophies and approaches of some of our **creative heroes**. Once we find ideologies that resonate, it often becomes easier to define our own unique approaches.[16]

> UX researcher and humanity-in-tech warrior
> **Vivianne Castillo** lives her professional life looking
> for opportunities to choose courage over comfort.[17]
> "What's hard about ethical imperatives is they're not
> often popular, common, or familiar," shares Castillo.
> "It's easier *not* to put in the work to productively call out
> something racist or sexist, so I remind myself of Brené
> Brown's wisdom that we can't have courage and comfort
> at the same time, and I advocate for better."[18]

Be an ethics educator

We can be mindful of opportunities to gently educate clients, partners, and colleagues and to empower them to act in ways that align with a greater purpose than the bottom line. One of the most powerful places to start—because capitalism—is by informing those around us about the sometimes-surprising business benefits of ethically driven pursuits.

Here are some helpful facts:

- ▶ Social good initiatives are increasingly embraced by consumers.[19]

- ▶ Companies that communicate a strong and meaningful purpose often realize increased brand loyalty.[20]

- ▶ 88 percent of folks are more likely to buy a product from a purpose-driven company.[21]

- ▶ Eco-friendly programs often save companies money by reducing waste and improving efficiencies.[22]

These are just a handful of helpful back-pocket examples that can support our efforts to educate our colleagues and clients about the quantifiable merits of making responsible choices.

Go public with your purpose

There are innumerable avenues to share our passions for ethical practice. We might mentor students in our industries and get involved with local college and university programs. We can take on the responsibility of getting the new intern up to speed. We can volunteer with local industry organizations; take on speaking gigs at conferences; be present at portfolio night; write for industry publications; have more face-to-face conversations. No matter how we do it, let's choose to have a voice in the greater creative community— each interaction is an opportunity to share philosophies and find our allies.

Don't expect to solve the problem

Let's collectively exhale as we release ourselves from the crushing responsibility of having to solve the world's most complex systemic problems. The age-old and arguably paternalistic notion of the single-handed "creative expert" is a thing of the past.

Though many of us have been told over the course of our creative lives that our roles are synonymous with problem solving, we now know a little better. The hubris of assuming we can solve the world's problems can lead to the work of creative industries becoming a figurative band-aid (at best) and an involuntary exacerbator (at worst). Instead, we can be content with a goal to respectfully research the problem, aim to accurately present its issues, and engage the public to promote meaningful, ongoing dialogue and action toward deeply collaborative incremental change.[23]

Co-create and collaborate

In an age of gurus, experts, thought leaders, coaches, and an emphasis on top-down power structures, it can be refreshing to gather a group of peers together for egalitarian collaboration. Collaboration is powerful when facilitated skillfully. Even when clients think they want to hire us as "creative experts," to come in and tell everyone else what we think they should do, we can show up and demonstrate our creative expertise in ways that favour supportive co-creation and balanced power dynamics. Think direct interfacing instead of assumptions, collaboration instead of cubicles, participatory community-wide workshop sessions instead of single-organization brainstorms, and personal connection with relevant populations instead of impersonal surveys and traditional focus groups. This shift in perception about the role of the creative will empower us to develop more inclusive and supportive interventions that genuinely leverage the experiences and knowledge of the very people we aim to support.

Rally your colleagues

Effective collaboration is best fuelled by free food—it's a known fact that rallying the team can be as simple as a "free lunch" subject line. Request a budget and offer healthy, tasty food in exchange for the attention of colleagues for a workshop focused on improving the company's ethical practices. Whether the focus is equitable hiring practices, diversity and inclusion, sustainable sourcing, responsible experience design, group volunteerism, or supporting the health and well-being of fellow employees, we can run meetings ourselves or invite local organizations or subject-matter experts to help us out. Non-profits, purpose-driven suppliers, and social enterprises are often more than happy to collaborate to support like-minded endeavours in exchange for visibility, support, or potential future partnerships.

Predefine your hard *no*

The choice to be fully engaged in our roles as conscious creatives will inevitably lead us to ethical dilemmas in our work. It is best practice to decide in advance what we will and will not work on with the people we report to. However, as we've covered, compromise *can* be necessary. Often the most beneficial thing we can do is accept a project and work hard (if our minds and bodies allow) to subvert from within. Perhaps the client is a weapons manufacturer, cigarette company, or fashion house known to exploit child labour; declining their work may be the only option our values system can handle. If that's the case, we might consider sending the client or our employer a short and respectful email outlining our reason for declining the work and reinforcing any previous agreement about our ethical stance. Not only does communicating our decision create an opportunity to educate, but it also protects our position. If we're feeling motivated, it's safe to do, and it doesn't compromise our job security (unless we're cool with that), we might satisfy our inner advocate by going public and speaking out about the unethical practices of the company in question.

Craft a list of ethical goals

We can start by asking: Does my creative collective, freelance practice, or organization have a set of ethical goals? Does my web design business have a social impact mission? Does my marketing team work actively to be more inclusive? Are my sustainability targets visible to the people who buy my stained glass art? Do my editors know that I am up-to-date on current issues in responsible journalistic practice? More than likely, there's a project ready to be adopted. Consider that this book may be a resource to start carefully selecting a set of actionable goals.

Be a resource

We may already be the office go-to source for *90 Day Fiancé* gossip (relatable, or is this just me?), but let's also position ourselves as resident experts on ethical practice. Who says we can't be all things? Let's stay current on the issues relating to our corner of the creative industries and the people who work there; we can have studies, articles, and books ready to share when colleagues express interest. We might consider writing a weekly or monthly newsletter. We can keep our real or figurative office doors open to anyone, at any level, internally and across the industry, for questions and support relating to responsible practice.

Witnessing a lack of action from leadership? Introduce colleagues to the change-making, internally subverting activism of groups like Amazon Employees for Climate Justice or the over 20,000 Google employees who walked out in protest of the mishandling of sexual harassment complaints. Teams at Microsoft, Apple, and Salesforce have also shown the power of petitions, strikes, and walkouts to demand accountability and change from their employers on issues like doing business with oil and gas companies, selling facial recognition software to police, and problematic contracts with immigration and customs enforcement.

Self-initiate ethical projects

If values-based work isn't possible in our day jobs, we might consider recruiting like-minded colleagues to collaborate outside of office hours. Let's forget the notion that clients are necessary to make ideas happen and pursue self-directed projects built around advocacy.[24] We might start our own non-profit, launch an ethical product, run workshops to co-create improved methods of activating communities, or contribute to purpose-driven publications.

Make *professional* ethical

The word *professional* can have problematic implications. At times, it can be interpreted as a synonym for a corporate drone or dispassionate employee maintaining the status quo until the clock strikes 5:00 p.m. or a person who mindlessly carries out company work while detaching from personal beliefs, and ethical and political values.[25] We've all seen it.

Rejecting that definition of professionalism means continuing to advocate for our values even during the work-day and allowing morality to drive our lives both personally *and* professionally.

Flag problematic projects

Fair, it's not always easy to be "that person," but here I am suggesting that it's worth it. As creative people, we're often involved in the early and pivotal phases before a project launches or before a product is ready for the sales team. As the team members involved early on, we can act as gate-keepers who voice concerns and advocate against ethically questionable products or services before they go to market.

Ask questions. Lead discussions. Generate consciousness around the issues at hand. Is a creative solution exclusionary? Misleading? Emotionally exploitative? Discriminatory? We might not always stop the project from moving forward, but we can generate critical awareness among all team members and throughout our networks and organizations.

Model conscious behaviour

Regardless of our role within an organization, our behaviour is always on display. Whether that visibility feels like a threat or an opportunity, we might consider asking: Am I behaving and speaking in ways that are inclusive? Am I careful to use a person's correct pronouns? Are my purchase decisions as ethical as possible? How responsible are my transportation choices? Do I proudly carry my reusables? Am I outspoken about current issues? Do I actively participate in local politics? How sustainable are my creative interventions? Are the projects I assign rooted in responsible citizenship? Nearly every decision is an opportunity to be a role model of conscious choices.

Read up

Ethical practice is no longer on the fringes of industry.
It is exploding across channels like Medium, Twitter, and
innumerable industry publications, as well as in the news.
Consider setting up a Google Alert (or use an alternative,
such as the online listening tool Awario or social media
search engine Social Searcher) to get updates on topics
such as moral philosophy and applied ethics, design ethics,
sustainability, social justice, conscious consumerism, social
innovation, inclusivity, accessibility, universal design, intersectional feminism, environmental justice, climate action,
more accountable forms of capitalism, and more.

Seek out companies with shared values

Across industries, people are increasingly seeking out companies whose missions are infused with purpose and meaning; consumers and employees alike have high ethical standards, demand equitable treatment, and are looking for opportunities to become a part of something bigger than themselves.[26]

With profit increasingly taking a back seat to purpose, the time is right to seek out businesses whose leaders are legitimately committed to supporting our values-based initiatives. Real talk: This isn't always easy. Product design manager Ailsa M. Blair shares that they have a number of companies on their resumé for whom they have led diversity and inclusion initiatives but only one whose leaders actually supported it.[27] Advocating for ethical and inclusive practice can be a demoralizing uphill climb without organizational support. Ailsa suggests doing research before joining an organization by interviewing employees and meeting up with folks connected to the network to make sure there is alignment between what is promoted publicly and what happens behind closed doors.

Get loud about your ethical intentions

By making our ethical intentions central to our communication efforts, both internal and external, we can become drivers of awareness for the conscious creative movement. Depending on our personality, though, this can be a tough task. We can challenge ourselves to interpret the idea of promoting our ethical intentions as different from bragging or shameless self-promotion. (For the record, shameless self-promotion is also entirely acceptable.) By sharing our intentions with the world, we recruit support for our mission and increase our potential for impact. Studies have shown that people actually *want* to hear about social and environmental achievements[28]—so don't be afraid to get loud.

Make your methods open-source

A core ethical practice that I recommend is operating from a position of generosity. This doesn't mean giving away our hard work for free; however, it can mean making certain tools, creative assets, and methods open-source or freely available to use under a Creative Commons license. Offering free-for-use workshop support, research, or visuals can be a method of promoting our work while supporting others and empowering anyone, regardless of economic position, to benefit from our privilege and knowledge.

Be community-minded

In her book *Good: An Introduction to Ethics in Graphic Design*, Lucienne Roberts wisely wrote, "The first step toward trying to be ethical is being socially aware and engaged."[29] An effective conscious creative is, first, an active community member. Ensuring we understand community needs from the inside is an amazing way to ensure we're not developing projects with a hierarchical, exclusive mentality. Attend community meetings. Stay informed and active in local politics. Volunteer. Have more conversations—including with people with whom you suspect you don't agree. Ask people what matters to them. Every chat is an opportunity to better understand the hopes and needs of the people we call neighbours and will invariably inform our collective creative output.

Connect to social innovation networks

Design for Social Innovation Towards Sustainability (DESIS) is a values-based non-profit cultural association and network of research labs largely based in academic institutions. Its purpose is to use the power of **social innovation** as a driver toward sustainable change, and its aim is to innovate around social demands instead of the demands of the market. Radically inclusive, evenly distributed, and non-hierarchical, these research labs value diverse expertise and subscribe to the belief that everyone can be (and should be) a designer of improved systems. We can connect with the network to learn more about this emerging philosophy, partner with a local lab, or find out how to get involved in social innovation initiatives in our communities.[30]

> **Social innovation** is the participatory development and implementation of programs that address systemic social and environmental issues with an overarching goal of strengthening civil society. Check out Participedia, a global community dedicated to sharing knowledge about public participation and democratic innovation; CitizenLab, a civic engagement platform that helps users co-create their city; Plume Labs, an organization whose mission is to make accurate air quality information accessible and empowering; and creative publics organization MASS LBP, which champions citizen deliberation and policy-making.[31]

Do the work you wish to see in the world

Self-initiate.
Seek out supportive resources.
React to local and global issues.
Start creating.

When (and if) free time allows, let's actively create the work we wish clients would pay us for to benefit causes that most require our support. We'll build our portfolios and accumulate a vital network of ethically minded conscious creatives.

Get vocal

An essential attribute of a conscious creative is a finely tuned "injustice radar" and a willingness to call out the issues it detects. Let's aim to be as vocal as possible about the causes we believe in. Speak up in person and online—across social media, in organizational communications, in marches and protests, and, arguably most importantly, in respectful and empathetic face-to-face conversations with folks whose belief systems may feel unfamiliar.

Any small step toward expression is worthy. Try to mitigate fear that public actions will negatively impact your career path. If we are honest and respectful in our public communication, we'll be certain to attract the organizations and companies we want to work with and, ideally, filter out the ones we don't.

Embrace peaceful resistance

There can be an incongruity between peaceful ideals and the violent-looking, radical images used to communicate messages in some activism circles. Consider that effective activism doesn't always promote tempestuous clashes of power but can resist in a way that makes use of action, language, and visuals that are non-violent. We can create resistance materials and support designed to promote collaborative, respectful relationships with the folks our messages aim to address. By doing so, we're more likely to foster the dialogue and open-mindedness that is essential for inciting change.

Get political

It can be argued that a person's vote is more valuable than anything they can do on the job, whether that job is as a creative or not.[32] Everyone's political actions matter. Stay informed. Read the news. Watch the debates. Sign up voters. We can improve our chances at living as responsible, active citizens by knowing where we stand on political issues locally and globally, and engaging where possible.

Align your career with your values

For some of us, full-time employment in a corporate organization may not be possible if we are to stay true to our ethical ideals. Instead, if we are able, we may choose to work as a freelancer, within a collective or co-op, with a social enterprise, or in the progressive non-profit sector. There are innumerable options for conscious creatives outside of traditional corporate roles.

Use your creative superpowers

Everyone can do something, but as creatives we have particular superpowers like storytelling, visualizing, lateral thinking, and creating moving and delightful experiences that have the power to change minds. Using our creative superpowers can be as simple as creating content that illuminates critical issues or as in-depth as conducting co-creation workshops to radically transform the way an organization, community, or even country operates. Our unique sets of practical and conceptual skills can take our ethical roles far beyond resistance against systems we perceive as unjust. We have the capacity to create the sorts of innovative, transformational ideas that can change how people live. Further, we can reimagine the methods of expressing those ideas in uniquely disruptive and breakthrough ways.[33]

Go pro bono

Bills paid? Feeling generous? Sometimes the best way to get involved in our local communities is to volunteer our services for free. Compensation can come in many forms that don't involve the exchange of money. We can barter for services, develop our networks by working with charity boards of directors, secure future paid work or bidding privileges, receive invaluable testimonials, build our portfolios with work that aligns with our values, and cultivate industry credibility. Whether we're just starting out or making a late-in-the-game switch toward conscious creative work, doing values-based work free of charge can benefit people in our communities while we support our own career goals. If it becomes a struggle to know where to donate work, consider instituting a grant process whereby organizations submit an application that outlines their needs. This process can help us evaluate who will most benefit from our support.

Say no to unethical clients

To be so uncompromising in our values that we turn down jobs from unethical clients (and, of course, subsequently advocate for changes to their practices) may be among the most challenging actions. Saying no to those offering to pay us can be difficult to impossible, depending on our situations, even when we see clearly that their practices grossly misalign with our ethics. Being able to afford to say no is a significant privilege. Establishing a low-cost, low-impact lifestyle is one way to support the likelihood that periodic blacklisting will be available to us.

On the bright side, the accountability and ethics of many industries are undergoing a significant shift at this point in history. Securing an ethical client base without significant compromise may be easier now than it has ever been.

Downsize your lifestyle

Let's call it like it is. Shifting our careers toward ethical pursuits can, at times, be financially burdensome. In order to support this transition, we might consider challenging ourselves to live a leaner lifestyle—what some call "living small." This action comes with a bold set of questions: What if we switched neighbourhoods? Lived in a smaller city? Sold our vehicles and instead took public transit or cycled when weather permitted? Made more of our own stuff? Grew our food? Created memories instead of buying things? It can be a disorienting, exciting, and deeply satisfying ongoing project to challenge the idea that success is determined materially.[34] Those of us living in high-income countries consume an astounding and entirely inessential amount of resources; there is plenty of room to reduce our impact, stay true to our values, and lead creatively fulfilling and comfortable lives.

Chapter
Two
Economic
Actions

Acknowledge your role in the system

Say it with me: "My name is _____ and I'm a tool of **capitalism**." A vital first step toward an ethical practice is owning our roles within a troublesome economy where consumption is king (or queen, or a gender neutral royal title yet to be determined) and the human, animal, and environmental consequences that come along with that. Being aware of the impact of the systems within which we operate can empower us with an enriched understanding of the work that we do and, hopefully, help us advocate for change. There is a fine line between being aware of issues and being crushed by the weight of the systemic problems we face. Aim for the former to stay in a headspace of action and empowerment, and remember, we can't single-handedly save the world with one profound act. What we *can* do is implement some of the actions outlined in this book, and develop some of our own, to effect incremental change toward a more equitable world.

> The dominant economic system of the Western world, **capitalism** is defined by *Merriam-Webster* as "private or corporate ownership of capital goods, by investments that are determined by private decision, and by prices, production, and the distribution of goods that are determined mainly by competition in a free market."[1]
>
> Contemporary or "late-stage" capitalism has been implicated in compromising the habitability of our planet and contributing to rising inequality, a suffering working class, structural unemployment, and a weakening of the political centre.[2]

Redefine your bottom-line ambitions

Success is measured by the size of our salaries, right? Many creative industries (advertising and tech, I'm looking at you) are rooted in a "more is more" mentality when it comes to cash.[3] To establish a conscious creative practice with ethics at its core sometimes requires a shift; priorities of abundant financial compensation are often replaced by those focused on the potential for impact and more balanced earning expectations. In expanding our purpose beyond bottom-line ambitions, we have to rethink our criteria for success. This doesn't mean we can't earn a comfortable living, but sometimes it means earning less in order to achieve more. Social impact organizations have less money for salaries than **unicorn start-ups**. Environmentally responsible projects aren't usually funded like oil and gas. I won't lie to you, there is often less money in purpose-based work, but benefits like enacting meaningful change, gaining job satisfaction, and living our values make it entirely worthwhile. Bonus, most organizations that centre responsible practice will also centre the well-being of their staff. That means we can kiss ableist ideas about intensive working hours, aggressive environments, and unhealthy conditions goodbye.

> A **unicorn start-up**, named for its statistical improbability, is a privately held company valued at over one billion U.S. dollars. The term was coined in 2013 by Aileen Lee. Airbnb, Uber, and Lyft are examples. (Lyft is technically a "decacorn," valued at over ten billion U.S. dollars.)

Advocate for living wages

Fact: Creative industries (most industries?) have a long history of treating their interns terribly. The worst offence? Not paying them at all. Exploitative and arguably elitist, since only those privileged enough to afford to work for free can accept such roles, unpaid internships are quickly becoming a thing of the past. We can advocate within our organizations for a collective understanding that everyone's time is valuable and that hiring talent in equitable ways for a fair **living wage** is the only acceptable choice. A conscious creative ensures all colleagues, regardless of seniority, are compensated fairly for their talents.

> **Different from minimum wage, a living wage reflects the minimum income a person requires to satisfy the actual costs of living in a specific region.**
>
> **A living wage for small families varies across cities in Canada and the U.S., but in major cities like Montreal, New York City, or Toronto, at the time of writing, living wages varied between approximately seventeen and thirty-one dollars per hour. Calculate living wages at livingwage.mit.edu and livingwagecanada.ca.**

Pitch the power of purpose

It's old news that sex sells. The new-ish news is that the ethical intentions of big brands and organizations do too. A huge percentage of consumers—92 percent, according to one study[4]—are so conscious about the impacts of their food, clothes, product, and service choices that they would switch brands for something with a more compelling purpose. Armed with the knowledge that purpose motivates people to financially support a company or make a purchase, let's urge our clients and collaborators to infuse a layer of social or environmental impact or animal rights into the projects we're a part of.[5] If we're working with supplied market data that doesn't include any psychographic information about our audience's penchant for purpose, we can do our own research and supplement where necessary. Like the great Dana Scully once said, the truth is out there.

Advocate against spec work

Near-universally condemned as unethical by innumerable creative organizations and industry authorities, spec work is the great under-valuer of the creative professions. We've been advocating against it since the dawn of time, and yet many creatives and agencies are still required to give away work for free in order to secure clients or contracts.

Beyond losing money and time on bids that don't pan out, spec work often means a rushed and informal creative process that can compromise the quality of work. It can also establish unfair and ineffective client/creative relationships, and all too often, it puts creative work at the risk of being plagiarized.[6] Further, spec is often solicited without a proper consultation or brief which can mean a lack of strategy, mediocre creative, and the perpetuation of practices such as contests in lieu of hiring professionals and fully engaging in the creative process. The truth is working on spec is bad for everybody's bottom line. It drains time and resources from a firm's paying clients and negatively affects clients by compromising the potential for long-term relationships.

When faced with a client expecting spec work, consider pitching the job without including the expected speculative creative work. Instead, include a short, respectful letter outlining why the practice is problematic. Challenging and brazen as it may be, it is also an excellent way to determine if the client is worthy of you or not. Taking that a step further, we might consider firing up our inner activist to go beyond simply declining spec work. We might get vocal in social media, report spec-soliciting clients to industry authorities, and join industry advocates already campaigning successfully against it.[7]

Measure your ethical successes

We live in an age of data obsession. For better or worse, we've created a world entirely preoccupied by quantifying and measuring the effectiveness of almost every move we make. Emerging areas like social impact, social innovation, sustainability, and various ethics-focused fields of creative practice haven't been around long enough to amass a great deal of data and case studies to support their successes.

Creatives are not always the most data-hungry folks around the table—I know I'm not—but sometimes we have to play along in order to prove our worth. We can help justify the value of prioritizing ethics by making a commitment to defining goals, reporting progress, and building supportive qualitative and quantitative data sets where possible.[8]

Speak in numbers

Advocating for anything from within a business or organization works most effectively when we're speaking the same language as the key decision makers. The same is true when we're advocating for an enhanced ethical practice. Before making the case, we can ask ourselves: What's in it for the business? Will it save them money? Bolster their reputation? Forge strategic partnerships?

Use the language of business and talk dollars.

As we've covered, there is no shortage of proof that consumers are increasingly attracted to businesses that embrace a responsible role as it relates to social and environmental impact. This often means reduced budgets, less waste, increased loyalty in customer bases, and more efficient employees.[9] Let's share our passion for the idea that making money while doing good is entirely possible, and educate ourselves and our employers on ideas about more **accountable** forms of capitalism.[10]

> The **Accountable Capitalism Act**, led by Elizabeth Warren, argues that if corporations claim legal rights of personhood, then they must also accept the moral obligations of personhood—that means corporations must become entities concerned with social and environmental issues, not just turning a profit.

Make ethics a competitive edge

It is measurably proven that public companies that *show* their ethical stance regarding factors such as climate change, labour rights, and public health are actually more stable and profitable than those whose visible focus rests solely on the bottom line.[11] That's a big deal. Discerning consumers are more loyal to organizations with shared values, so things like social responsibility are a legitimate competitive edge in business.

Further, employees are drawn to purposeful businesses. Purpose improves talent retention and incentivizes clients and consumers to pay a premium for products and services. It's clear why many business leaders argue that corporate social responsibility (CSR) is essential to the success of every organization.[12]

Help for-profits support non-profits

Traditional pro bono is great, but what if our for-profit clients could support us to donate even more work to companies that really need it? Named one of the one hundred most influential creatives working today, Matthew Manos, founder and managing director of the agency verynice developed a "give half" model, where half of the work they do is given away for free to companies that otherwise wouldn't be able to afford quality creative work.[13] They fund this through traditional work for corporate clients who understand that by employing verynice, they're contributing to both the greater good and their own often-profitable CSR initiatives. And of course, in line with their generous approach, the give-half model is open-source. Everybody wins.[14]

Choose your causes wisely

In the same way we assess potential clients, it is essential to research the practices of the causes and charities we may potentially support or collaborate with. Since transparency is a legal requirement for all non-profits, their annual reports are readily available for our critical perusal. An easier place to start, however, is with Charity Intelligence in Canada or Charity Navigator in the U.S.[15] These third-party organizations are dedicated to **reviewing non-profits** for the quality of their impact, allocation of donation money, need for funding, accountability to donors, and overall financial transparency. The next time an iPad-wielding charity ambassador stops us on the sidewalk or a project request pops into our inbox, we can inquire about that charity's rating before deciding where our time or money goes. Research tip: Investigate potential misalignments in politics to ensure we're not inadvertently supporting an organization which has projected an image of benevolence during crisis, engaging in "coronawashing" acts of empty lip service to frontline workers while doing nothing to reorganize access to resources, or has historically discriminated against marginalized folks like the LGBTQ2IA+ community (I'm looking at you, Salvation Army[16]).

> If you're looking for a partner and don't know where to start, many charity rating sites boast Top 10 or Top 100 lists. If animal testing is a potential risk factor, as it can be in the case of medical organizations, assess your potential partner at Humane Charities Canada or Animal Charities of America.[17]

Instill gratitude in audiences

Whether we use video, performance, writing, digital experiences, or advertising, for those of us whose creative work helps to secure donations to purpose-driven organizations, messages about gratitude make a huge impact. Research shows that reminding people about who and what helped them along their path to success increases feelings of gratitude and empathy for those who didn't have similar support.[18] This can be a helpful insight for creating effective communication and visual support in the non-profit space to motivate increased donations and participation.

Apply for grants

Awarded by governments, institutions, corporations, or the foundations of wealthy individuals or families, lots of grant money exists to help creative folks fund for-good initiatives. A quick online search will yield lists of grant opportunities by location, by area of focus, or for specific demographics. To apply for grants, we must start with a compelling proposal that outlines a mission, an approach, a plan to measure success and end with a submission (and then cross our fingers and hope for the best). Grant writing is an art that takes time to perfect, so aim to be persistent and avoid getting discouraged—even the most seasoned grant writers get declined sometimes. Looking for a less intensive application process? Consider applying for microgrants: These are smaller, non-repayable sums of money awarded by groups of local donors.

Sell environmental stewardship

Like the earth, climate action is so hot right now. It is proven that clients and consumers alike react favourably to intentions to address the damage we've done to the planet and mitigate further abuse. Fun fact: The average consumer has been shown to be more attracted to spending their cash with companies that acknowledge and address their environmental impact. Armed with this knowledge, conscious creatives can encourage clients to explicitly weave their environmental action plans and messages into the work.[19] Another fact: Companies with climate action plans are proven to be more financially stable and attractive to investors. With a proven bottom-line benefit, there's no good reason that an organization shouldn't hear us out and agree to champion environmental stewardship.[20]

Insist on a triple bottom line

"Working to a triple bottom line" means that we consider the social and environmental and economic impacts of our work, and so do our employer and our networks of clients and suppliers. Insisting that every project begins with measurable objectives that include this triple bottom line can ensure that a company's financial needs and decisions don't compromise its social and environmental goals.[21]

Consider a quadruple bottom line

If we're feeling particularly keen, we might follow the lead of design for sustainability leader and philosopher Stuart Walker, who argues to expand the measure of the triple bottom line beyond the social, environmental, and economic impacts to include personal fulfillment. He argues that **the path to sustainability** starts at the individual level where a focus on personal meaning-seeking is critical to developing the perspective and conscience necessary to realize an ethical practice.[22]

> If unsure about how to approach this undertaking, we can consider using the **quadruple bottom line** as a way to sort and assess our business plans, creative solutions, resources, and challenges; it also makes a good organizing principle for group meetings, reports, and even book manuscripts.

Capture true costs

Listen, I ride the struggle bus all the way to math town too, but accounting gets us paid. The nerdy sibling of the triple bottom line, true cost accounting is an approach that ethical creatives and the businesses they're involved with can benefit from.[23] It ensures environmental, social, and economic impacts are identified, quantified, and made transparent. By accurately reporting on the holistic impacts of an initiative, organizations can be sure that future projects account for more than just economic costs. By doing so, they ensure a line of sight into any potentially damaging aspects of their business. As creatives, we may not always be expected to crunch the numbers, but knowing what to advocate for is crucial.

Trade, barter, and share

I would argue that resourcefulness is in the blood of creative folks. Trading with colleagues or sharing resources such as physical supplies and technology can save our hard-earned money and reduce our overall impact. We can participate in barter groups like Bunz or visit consignment and second-hand stores.[24] Of course, we'll eventually have to buy some supplies to support the work we do, so it's best to ask ourselves first whether something is essential. When a purchase is necessary, well-researched decisions can save us from making a takes-500-years-to-break-down landfill contribution or supporting manufacturing practices that have dire environmental consequences.

Many of us are Apple users, so we'll be pleased to know that Greenpeace named Apple among the most eco-friendly companies globally.[25] Apple is committed to sustainable practices, but it's still working to stop the environmentally destructive mining of rare earth metals to make its technologies. As ethical consumers of products, we can stay connected to the environmental initiatives of the companies we support and do what we can to keep them accountable to their goals.[26]

Get into Creative Commons

As conscious creatives, we tend to be generous, open-source kinds of people whose more-the-merrier ideals celebrate free access to resources and information. Creative Commons (CC) licenses enable free distribution and usage of creative assets that other folks can share, use, build upon, and distribute too.[27] Getting into the CC community saves us money, supports a sharing culture, and democratizes assets and information. With sixteen variations of licenses, we can stipulate terms, like requiring attribution if someone uses our work or only allowing users the right to distribute the work if its purpose is non-commercial.

"We must do our own personal work as well as contribute to changing practices and policies within wider systems."

Chapter Three
Social Actions

Cultivate empathy

Connecting to the needs and aspirations of others is crucial to socially conscious creative projects. Empathy has been described as a state that "requires us to put aside our learning, culture, knowledge, opinions, and worldview purposefully in order to understand other peoples' experiences of things deeply and meaningfully."[1] This applies as much to our audiences as it does to our colleagues, clients, employees, and students.

Conscious creatives can tap into our empathy as a tool to enhance our understanding and capacity to connect with our collaborators and audiences. We can take this a step further. By committing to deep research, we can unearth insights that, when effectively shared in the messages we infuse our projects with, can gently nudge our audiences to tap into their own empathetic selves. We can, thereby, instill heightened levels of compassion, understanding, and connection in the folks engaging with our projects.

Start small in social impact

The social impact space can be riddled with life's big questions, and it's easy to get overwhelmed by seemingly unsolvable, intensely complex problems. A good place to start is to *try* not to get weighed down with the gravity of the problems society faces. We can start small. Contribute at a local level with the people we know and trust. Approach our projects one step at a time, starting with the concerns of our local communities. Work collaboratively to make change where we can. If we're still feeling motivated once we have tackled local-level problems, we can move on to the global initiatives.[2]

Get obsessed with accessibility

The numbers are no joke. Over 4.4 million people in Canada and 61 million in the United States are considered disabled. That means a whopping one in four Americans lives with some sort of disability—some are visible, some are not. With an ageing population, this number is only set to rise.[3] It is an absolute necessity for any ethical creative practitioner to ensure that our creative output is as accessible as it can be. We can begin by familiarizing ourselves with the accessibility resources available through government and industry bodies found in the Resources section (see page 203), including government accessibility standards, Web Content Accessibility Guidelines, accessible fonts, **descriptive text**, universal access symbols, and the principles of inclusive and universal design.

> **Accessibility in action: Everyday creators are beginning to use descriptive text in social media posts. Descriptive text, also known as alt text, shared alongside an image post, enables the description of that image to be read by software used by the visually impaired. Because, real talk, everyone deserves to experience your astrology memes.**

Accessible creative output and practice should also be inclusive. An important aspect of creative inclusivity is ensuring that a diverse set of decision makers are represented throughout the process of working on a project. That means people with differing abilities—physical, cognitive, mental health, et cetera—support key creative decision making throughout. Live by the mantra popularized in 1990s disability activism: "Nothing about us without us."

Champion inclusivity

The truth is that discourse in the creative industries has been largely dominated by **cisheteropatriarchal Anglocentric/Eurocentric** ways of knowing, seeing, and acting in the world.[4] In other words, the groups of practitioners talking about design, architecture, tech, and the like have been pretty homogenous—cisgender, straight, male, and white. As a conscious creative, it's crucial to get real with ourselves and see beyond Western perspectives. Let's actively seek to expand the richness of knowledge that influences our work.

> **Heteropatriarchy,** or **cisheteropatriarchy,** describes the sociopolitical system where heterosexual cisgender men have primacy over other sexual orientations and gender identities.
>
> **Anglocentric/Eurocentric** refers to a focus on English or European culture to the exclusion of other worldviews.

It bears repeating: In order to practice more inclusively, represent authentically, develop truly accessible output, and approach issues with a depth of understanding, we *must* aim to maximize the diversity of voices on project teams and start listening more deeply. We can actively notice cultural and experiential similarities and differences without making value judgements and be inquisitive when we encounter something we don't understand. We can work to understand the nuances that exist in a culture or subculture and respect the unique worldviews that result from those experiences, rituals, languages, religions, histories, and politics that differ from our own. Doing so will significantly increase our sensitivity as we interact with and represent people in our work. It can also mean the difference between perpetuating harmful, discriminatory practices and committing respectful and reconciliatory speech and action.[5]

Commit to reconciliation and decoloniality

For those of us *not* from historically oppressed peoples, this is a topic best approached with mindfulness of our own privilege and a commitment to park (indefinitely) any lingering **fragility**. Education, reconciliation, and decoloniality as they relate to the systemic oppression and genocide of racialized peoples, including Black and Indigenous communities, are complex and utterly crucial undertakings. Conscious creatives, especially white folks whose cultural histories are steeped in oppression, must commit to informing themselves about historical and contemporary injustice, systemic inequity, and the brutal generational ramifications of both. This knowledge is essential to creating work that centres social justice.

> **White fragility** is a term coined by U.S. academic and educator Robin DiAngelo to address the defensiveness, indignation, and discomfort that can occur when white people engage with racial injustice and inequality.

Unsure where to start? We can read more books, get connected to social justice organizations, and make efforts to dismantle the racist lens through which many of us experience the world. We can support networks with our time and talent, amplify voices, contribute financially, and promote opportunities for BIPOC (Black, Indigenous, and People of Colour), QTPOC (Queer and Trans People of Colour), and other marginalized groups. We can be mindful about the Indigenous histories of the land we occupy and learn to acknowledge it as such. We can ensure that our research, curriculums, and choices in creative inspiration are informed by Black and Indigenous knowledge as well as that of other communities whose histories and wisdom have been historically suppressed.

This short exploration of incremental actions cannot do justice to the severity and complexity of the issues they attempt to address. I implore all of us to continuously work toward a deeper understanding of **reconciliation**, social justice, decoloniality, and the brutality of the social, economic, and physical violence repeatedly committed in the name of white supremacy and colonization.

> **The word reconciliation entered the vernacular in recent years largely because of the Truth and Reconciliation Commission of Canada. Due to the government's failure to make any significant progress on the Commission's ninety-four calls to action, the word has taken on a pejorative connotation. For many, more useful terms to express the transformative change we wish to see include decoloniality, decolonization, and equity.**

Some celebrated books on the topic include *Elements of Indigenous Style*, *The New Jim Crow*, *We Should All Be Feminists*, *White Fragility*, *Bad Feminist*, and *All Our Relations*.

Call out the "ists" and the "phobes"

Calling out racist, ageist, ableist, homophobic, transphobic, fatphobic, or sexist behaviour, regardless of where it's coming from, is an absolute imperative for the ethical practice of a conscious creative. Whether we inform HR, leadership, a colleague, or, ideally, whoever is uttering the problematic language, when we are witness to discriminatory behaviour, it is our responsibility, as long as it is safe to do so, to speak up and advocate for it to stop.

Perhaps just as important is having a voice as it relates to the socially responsible actions we witness. Let's publicly celebrate the ethical "glow-ups" of our colleagues, clients, and suppliers who are making changes to their practices by taking action against injustice and improving conditions for all people.

Leading by example is great, but let's not be afraid to speak up about our own ethical actions. A well-promoted conscious creative practice can be a memorable point of difference that advances the collective movement toward responsible approaches to work as well as our individual career goals.

Rethink retouching

Photoshopping is so ubiquitous that, like Kleenex, it has
become a proprietary eponym independent of its Adobe
roots. Designers and non-designers alike know what
it represents: The removal of imperfections, so-called
beautification, enhancement of perceived assets, and the
improvement of saleability—often at the expense of authentic representation. Heavily retouched, impossibly perfected
images of human bodies can have a negative effect on body
image and mental health.[6] In recent years, however, a handful of organizations have publicly banned the retouching
of their models to reflect a more honest, accurate image of
real people to their viewers.[7] Sure, the data has yet to show
whether this has a positive impact on sales, but unretouched
imagery has been unequivocally met with love and appreciation by audiences who are tired of unrealistic bodies filling
their feeds. I, for one, am here for it.

Watch your words

Let's collectively commit to never using language that is violent, racist, misogynistic, homophobic, transphobic, body-shaming, or ableist or language that risks activating traumatic memories in the folks around us.

A few pro tips: Avoid posting explicit discussion of traumatic topics like eating disorders, sexual assault, war and violence, or phobias and medical procedures without a content or trigger warning (often denoted using CW or TW). Ask and never assume to know a person's **pronouns** or gender identity (super pro tip: gender expression ≠ gender identity), and start meetings with new folks by introducing yourself along with your own pronouns to get the ball rolling.

> **Some group facilitators and instructors request that all participants share their preferred names and their pronouns ahead of time to avoid having trans folks feel vulnerable or exposed during an introduction. This can be especially important when working with youth.**

Don't stereotype based on race (or anything else, for that matter). Don't default a person's gender in every hypothetical situation to *he*. Don't call things *gay* (unless you're watching a particularly *sickening* episode of *RuPaul's Drag Race*, and even then the intention needs to be celebratory and respectful—actually, just don't). Know the origins of the idioms you use so you're not inadvertently using sexist or racist references. Avoid using ableist words like *crazy*, *psycho*, *lame*, *dumb*, or *insane*.

We can take this conscious use of language a step further by avoiding fatphobic language when talking about other people's bodies or our own, and avoiding violent and militaristic turns of phrase that are often rife in business environments—think *target, war room, execution, interrogate, post-mortem, guerrilla tactics, blasting, pulling out the big guns, bait and switch, capture*…the list goes on. Inadvertently using violent language supports aggressive working environments and contributes to a culture of othering our audiences to create an "us versus them" mentality.

Reflect the actual population

Regardless of how ethically challenging our work environments are, there is often one thing we creatives maintain control over—representation in the work we create. We can choose to present balanced and honest depictions of people from a variety of or intersecting communities and backgrounds like racialized folks, the queer community and people with disabilities or bodily differences. Further, consider boldly challenging the standardized gender and ethnic assumptions that are so often supplied in personas and "target" market descriptions. If they are narrow, exclusionary, and inaccurately representative of the true composition of society, speak up. A word of caution: Avoid tokenism. Tokenism is the practice of making only a symbolic effort to give the appearance of equality or diverse representation. We can avoid this transgression by consulting with the people we represent, being consistently committed to supporting visibility and positive representation for diverse communities, and always advocating for and participating in larger systemic efforts toward true inclusivity.

Help your audience live in good (mental) health

Over the years, the creative industries have been complicit in manufacturing needs in all sorts of damaging ways. The practice of manipulating audience behaviour has become increasingly stealthy through the use of things like dark patterns, the repetitive hyper-targeting and re-targeting of ads and past-viewed products, and addictive experiences in digital product design. Aiming to identify and avoid these modes of practice is a key step toward an ethical practice.

I would argue that we can't be conscious creatives if we're exploiting self-esteem to sell a product; infusing fat-phobia into our marketing messages; advertising nutritionally void food to kids; producing experiences that capitalize on a dopamine/reward response; selling high fashion using violent, misogynistic imagery; or promoting mindless consumption. These ethical pitfalls aren't always simple to avoid; however, mindful awareness, positive intentions, and advocating for the promotion of healthy behaviours in our audiences are steps in the right direction.

Build purpose into office outings

We've all seen it: Leadership often loves a committee dedicated to company culture and fun (sometimes not-so-fun) team-building activities. Take the eye-roll out of forced fun by participating in an action that does some good. Consider partnering with a local (vetted) non-profit or community group to collectively volunteer support.

Examples include organizing shore cleanups, working at a local shelter or food bank, or helping build a home for a family in need. Not only can colleagues collaborate over shared values and develop deeper levels of self-awareness during these events, volunteering is also shown to improve employee engagement at work, which can positively impact revenue.[8] Further, the average worker isn't just in it for the money anymore. Studies of millennials, for example, show that employees are deeply motivated by altruism.[9] Consider how corporate volunteerism can support a socially aware career while fulfilling fellow employees and helping companies retain talent.

Create with transparency in mind

In a perfectly ethical world, creative output would be universally transparent. It wouldn't persuade, manipulate, coerce, or mislead but instead would reflect the absolute facts. Since we don't live in that world and ethical perfection is, arguably, an impossibility, we must learn to be as honest and transparent as possible *where possible*.

Let's set an intention to provide our audiences with the best chance of making an informed decision without the interference of misleading visuals, materials, or language. We can aim to maintain transparency through appropriate colour choice (especially when working on a brand that might veer into greenwashing territory) or imagery, ensure terms and conditions are clear and accessible, and avoid vague or inflated promotional terms. In cases where having an impact on claims or textual elements is impossible, we may use our unique creative sophistication to *show* the truth, even when language doesn't support our cause.[10] This may be implicit instead of explicit, but every little bit helps.

Amplify the underrepresented

Listen, not everyone is an activist. The frontlines are a special sort of place for a special sort of person. That's not me and that's okay. That *doesn't* mean I can't borrow some inspiration and learn to amplify in the way an activist typically does.

We can start by looking around and listening. Can we boost the signals of those fighting for employee rights? Can we speak up about the discrimination or underrepresentation we notice in our PTA meeting or Extreme Ironing group. (This is a real thing that has 5,000 likes on Facebook. What a time to be alive.) Can we advocate for those without a voice like our animal friends or the environment? Can we amplify the social media statements of oppressed groups to widen the reach of the message?

If we choose to take on a cause, it's crucial to remember that it's best practice, where possible, for the underrepresented group to lead. We can listen and facilitate without appointing ourselves as a **saviour**. Let's commit to providing support where it's requested and never, ever assume to understand a group's unique experiences.

> Go follow @**NoWhiteSaviors** and join their nearly 340,000 Instagram and 25,000 Twitter followers to get educated and help advocate against "the rampant abuses committed by white missionaries and development workers in Uganda and beyond." **nowhitesaviors.org/who-we-are/story.**

Create for empowerment, not exploitation

Among our highest motivations as humans are the needs to belong, feel loved, and be appreciated by our peers. Facebook is, arguably, among the biggest perpetrators of using creative power (design features) to exploit these motivations as psychological vulnerabilities. Succeeding in achieving its goal to consume (and monetize) as much of our time and conscious attention as possible, Facebook's introduction of the like button initiates a rush of dopamine (glorious social approval) that feels so good that users can't help but upload more stuff to get another hit.[11] And just like that, they're hooked. This is the same psychology behind platforms like TikTok, Snapchat, and Instagram and why they are so hard to break away from.

The lesson? Doing the right thing means designing so our audiences can make informed, empowered choices instead of acting on the urges of addiction. A great place to start is by learning the principles of behaviour design to better understand how it can be exploited at the expense of the user, and conversely how to use its principles for good.[12]

Create for maximum usability

Ensuring a high level of usability is essential to creating ethical experiences online and in the (so-called) real world. In the tech world, a lack of usability can, and often does, result in the use of **dark patterns**.[13] These ominous-sounding interface elements trick users into doing something they didn't want to do, like adding extras to a shopping cart or swiping[14] or clicking unintentionally.[15]

> **Dark patterns are just one way design encourages certain behaviours, often unconscious or compulsive, in users. Some consider them part of a troubling movement to intentionally get users addicted to digital products through incessant push notifications, endless scrolling, strategic and repeated content placement, slot machine–style loading experiences, and more. This addictive side of the internet is a bit like the layout of an IKEA or a casino—just with more cat videos.**

We can use the Neilson Norman Group's five quality components of usability to ensure that any experience we create for our audience is made based on best practices:

1. Learnability: The ease of accomplishing tasks on the first try

2. Efficiency: The speed at which users can perform tasks

3. Memorability: The speed to re-establish proficiency after a period of not using the design

4. Errors: Number of errors, severity, and ease of recovery from them

5. Satisfaction: How pleasant something is to use

Learn the legalities of web accessibility

The United Nations Convention on the Rights of Persons with Disabilities recognizes web accessibility as a human right.[16] As conscious creatives and citizens of the digital world, we have a responsibility to ensure that the experiences we create online adhere to the legal accessibility requirements of the cities, provinces, and countries in which we work. These requirements are often made available through our respective industry organizations, but we can also lean on government documents like the Accessibility for Ontarians with Disabilities Act (AODA). This law is among the most comprehensive summaries of proper web accessibility standards globally and its mission is to outline "the degree to which a product, device, service, or environment is available to as many people as possible."[17] Regardless of origin, the AODA is a resource to support accessible creation that complies with the highest standards. Pro tip: Check out the Web Content Accessibility Guidelines at W3.org for a comprehensive and practical guide to meeting accessibility standards.[18]

Push for data protection

Many of us create digital experiences, feature our work online, or sell our work through various platforms on the internet. That means we're participating in data collection of one type or another. Understanding the regulations around data protection is important to our roles as ethical creatives whose work aims to protect the rights of those around us. We can familiarize ourselves with the Personal Information Protection and Electronic Documents Act (PIPEDA) in Canada and its European equivalent, the General Data Protection Regulation (GDPR).[19] Each can support us in appropriately advocating for ethical practices any time data is gathered relating to our work. These regulations are legally binding, so if an organization breaches user rights, it can be fined. Basics to remember include the following: Users have the right to data portability and the right be forgotten; data collection can only be done with explicit consent; everyone has the right to access their data and the right to withdraw consent or delete accounts at any time.

Curb reflexive consumption

Consider the rabbit hole of endless scrolling that most of us have fallen victim to in our social apps of choice (are they still a choice?). Creative decisions like incorporating "bottomless flow" or autoplay keep people consuming well past the point of being hungry.[20] The same goes for crafting experiences that—as I mentioned above—apply the psychology of a slot machine to keep users persistently checking their devices for new notifications.[21] With innumerable studies linking excessive screen time to increased anxiety, depression, and even suicidal thoughts—especially in teens—it's imperative that we, as conscious creatives, support healthy relationships with devices.[22] We can aim to conclude experiences once the user has accomplished the task they set out to do, or consider giving users the power to determine specific times of day to receive notifications.

Get involved in humanizing tech

There is a growing community of industry leaders dedicating their careers to making sure that the stuff we create in the tech realm isn't doing unnecessary harm. They're raising awareness about, and actively creating solutions to mitigate, the ways that culture, business, design, and organizational structures can drive technology to hijack our brains. (As Douglas Coupland says, "I miss my pre-internet brain.") Educating ourselves and participating in the ongoing conversations led by Tristan Harris and the Center for Humane Technology, All Tech Is Human, and digital health communities can expand our ethical networks and inform advocacy in our creative practice.[23]

Advocate for net neutrality

The Canadian Radio-television and Telecommunications Commission (CRTC) defines net neutrality as the principle that all internet traffic should be given equal treatment by internet service providers (ISPs).[24] This means that as users, Canadians have full access to all online content and applications regardless of their source, without providers favouring or blocking particular products or websites (except of course when outside countries don't make their content accessible to us and I can't watch *Pose* on Netflix—life is hard).

Unlike in the U.S., in Canada it's illegal for ISPs to compromise user access. This doesn't mean, however, that the big telecom companies don't periodically push back. As recently as 2018, Canada's major telecom companies attempted to censor sites in order to fight piracy. This attempt at censorship was viewed by many as a slippery slope toward compromising net neutrality in the way that the American government has. The Canadian government unanimously voted that "a Canadian carrier shall not control the content or influence the meaning or purpose of telecommunications carried by it for the public."[25] So, for now, Canadian online space is transparent as ever, but it's up to all of us to stay connected to the cause, support the countries whose online space has been compromised, and advocate when necessary.

Show love to your atypical audiences

It has been said that the difference between universal and inclusive design is that inclusive design is not a result, it's a process.[26] Core to that process is the act of creating with the people for whom the product is intended.

Best practice includes paying special attention to the users who may have previously been excluded because they're considered "edge cases," or users with atypical needs or abilities. It's often impossible to predict the requirements of users whose needs differ from our own, so it's imperative to include those users in the creative process itself.

Help build citizenship-centric curriculums

At some point in our creative lives, many of us will become educators and develop curriculums. In doing so, we have a crucial choice. We can continue the tradition of assigning projects intended to single-mindedly hone a students' craft, or we can choose to assign work that cultivates critical social, political, and environmental awareness. We can motivate students to use their creative power to foster progressive change and reinforce that creative work can never be divorced from content.[27]

Once released to the world, our students' projects will, invariably, have very real ramifications. Let's equip them to become conscious creatives who can effectively navigate the ethical implications of the decisions they make in the real world.

Create equitable workplaces

Working with equity in mind means that we level the proverbial playing field of our workplaces and, generally, avoid being the sort of people who compromise other folks' opportunities to succeed. When we account for unique needs and differing abilities among employees, we take into account things like language barriers, cultural and learning differences, and visible and invisible health issues and disabilities. Let's provide our colleagues with supplemental support where it's needed most, stay informed on accessibility policies, and help people access the institutional or organizational help that they require. If there is no supplemental support to be found within our organization, let's advocate until there is.

Be an ethical citizen of the internet

With a pretty shocking number of our waking hours being spent online (one study claims we spend six hours and forty-two minutes online every day),[28] it's crucial to understand how to conduct ourselves ethically in digital spaces. A few questions to ask ourselves: Am I honouring others with my words and actions? Am I respecting copyrighted materials that belong to others? Am I ensuring my content is as accessible to as many people as possible? Am I citing my sources appropriately and crediting creators where necessary? Being an ethical citizen of the internet means keeping it legal, avoiding harming or embarrassing others, and never putting someone's personal information or intellectual property at risk.

Demand diverse teams

Whether we're the ones doing the hiring, advocating from within an organization, or having any impact on the makeup of the teams, clients, or suppliers, keeping our work community from becoming boring and homogenous lumps of uniformity has been *proven* to be essential to effectively generating social impact.

Studies show that in creative industries, responsible work is many times more likely to be made a priority by "women and minorities."[29] The creative work of systemically under-represented and stigmatized groups is affected by the unique experiences and power struggles they face. The result? An enhanced level of empathy and a passionate commitment to advocacy and ethical creative practice.[30]

Design a democratized workplace

By establishing equal investment in projects and company performance, a worker-run co-operative can lay the foundation for success in building a socially responsible, democratic, equitable business. Values-driven and hierarchy-free co-ops keep the decision-making power in the hands of their members and often engender a more engaged staff, increased productivity, and even enhanced potential for innovation.[31]

Hire people who "get it"

In a position to hire? In the world of conscious creativity, craft is nothing without a passion for purpose. Portfolios are important, but we can consider a 50/50 interview approach where hard skills are given as much weight as a candidate's fit within the ethical culture we're establishing. Let's aim to hire people whose lives are steeped in community participation, volunteerism, political engagement, and consciousness as it relates to social matters, animal welfare, and environmental issues.

Create safe and supportive spaces

The cultivation of an ethical, supportive work environment that is a **safe space** for all employees regardless of age, gender, sexuality, race, or ability is an essential aspect of conscious leadership. We can work to keep our values central to all interactions and ensure the office is a safe space in which to share any issue, from interpersonal conflict to mental health needs. We can lead by example with respectful, sensitive conduct, and a zero-tolerance policy on ethics violations. We can show up authentically, be open about our personal values and the problems we contend with, and encourage others to do the same.

We might provide workshops about ethical conduct and employee training about how to be a good ally. Actively praise ethical conduct. And finally, ensure there are protective mechanisms in place to support employees who encounter problems.[32] If humans are involved, issues will happen and people will get hurt. What matters is that our organizations are proactive and have established systems and HR supports in place to provide help when it is inevitably needed.

> Create **safe spaces** online too. Remember when @i_weigh and Instagram teamed up to protect kids under eighteen from being exposed to diet/detox products posted by irresponsible influencers? How about when Snapchat introduced a mental health tool that surfaced supportive resources if it detected sensitive search terms like *thinspo* (pro-anorexia content) or *depression*? If big social can make efforts to create safe spaces, so can the rest of us.

Keep the social in "social impact"

In her book *Citizen Designer*, Cheryl Heller says it simply and says it best when she expresses that the essential nature of social impact is that it's social. Community collaboration is the key to success if we're aiming to support people with our creative practice.

The easiest place to find our collaborators? We can get a job within an organization that has already taken up the causes we aspire to support.[33] Or, if we plan to freelance, we can get involved with other solo creatives, build our own teams, and make sure our practices remain active and rooted in community. We can consider joining local boards, offering internships, teaching locally, and volunteering whenever possible.

Consistent engagement within local governments and communities not only increases quality of life but also provides an insider understanding of the hopes, needs, and opportunities of the folks within a particular community.[34] And really—how can deeper understanding of communities do anything *but* positively impact our ability to make creative magic together?

Partner, don't parachute

Collaboration can be the difference between creating *for* and creating *with*. (Aim for the latter.) As conscious creatives, respectful immersion in a community is the most effective way to understand, incorporate, and mobilize the skills and strengths of its members and resources. This action can add a dimension of authenticity, accuracy, and empowerment to our work.[35]

Avoid the often-critiqued parachute style of social impact work: A well-intentioned but "paternalistic and misdirected" form of intervention that "parachutes" into high-need settings without taking time to understand the real problems faced by those people.[36] This method can be seen in some forms of "voluntourism" and can be especially prevalent in work for vulnerable populations in so-called developing nations. The ramifications of hastily chosen volunteers, poorly considered projects, and misunderstood or altogether ignored community needs and nuances can result in the reinforcement of othering, unsatisfactory work, increased dependency of vulnerable communities on external sources, and more extreme violations.

Represent with dignity

When using our creative skills to support social initiatives, we're often working to draw attention to the impact of injustices. It can be tempting to focus on the "victims" in these stories and their ostensible lack of power. I challenge us, however, to present dignified representations of individuals impacted by injustice. If we present issues in an intelligent, clear, and nuanced way while focusing on the strengths, resilience, and holistic humanity of the people we're working with, we can avoid compromising the integrity of our collaborators. Let's aim to identify and elevate the talents and strengths of the people we're tasked to represent. We can seek out uniqueness and power in cultural traditions, language, or skill sets.[37] By doing so, our interventions can educate and inspire change in our audiences without compromising anybody's dignity or empowerment.

Be mindful of literacy and language

Arguably, all creative work has a voice, and, in most cases, it shouldn't be that of the creative doing the work. Working at the same level of literacy, language, and cultural norms of the groups we create with is essential to representing responsibly and ensuring that our work is accessible.[38] This is where inclusive approaches to creativity come in. The best way to ensure we're speaking in a voice appropriate to our audience is to ensure that representatives of that audience are present throughout the process to share what works for them and what doesn't.

Create with legacy in mind

Put those generosity pants back on—in fact, just keep them on. Legacy is about making sure our creative projects can live on without us. Start by asking: How might this client and audience continue to benefit from my work when I am no longer present to implement or modify it? Creating with local community groups and non-profits often means smaller budgets, so it's entirely possible the client won't have the means to hire us again in the immediate future.

Ensuring our work's longevity means being creative about figuring out how that work can be easily replicated and modified without us. This may mean providing creative frameworks for implementation, crafting written method-ologies, or making projects using easily accessible and open-source software.

Consider that by giving our work a longer shelf life, we're not putting ourselves out of a job but instead being good partners and strengthening our relationships. By support-ing organizations generously, we're likely to obtain valuable referrals, get a call for the next project, and live our values all the while.

Design for democracy

Participation in democracy is fundamental to our agency and empowerment as citizens. And since it's been said that good creative work is good citizenship (paraphrasing Milton Glaser), we might ask what we can do to support our local democracy in functioning optimally for its leaders and constituents.[39] We can use the power of our creative skills to increase civic participation through things like designing ballots, advocating for voter turnout, and working to make government/citizen interactions easier to understand and more transparent. It's a deeply worthy cause for any of us interested in social impact.[40]

Share project ownership

Collaboration and shared ownership are core to developing the sort of strong, long-term, and mutually beneficial relationships that make community projects successful. Make sure the experiences of people within the communities you're working with are at the centre of your creative process—it is their insights, after all, that will enable the project to flourish.

Make it analogue

When creating to develop strong and connected communities, consider that reliance on or *defaulting* to a technology-based solution may not always serve our cause well. Social innovation leader Ezio Manzini believes that a community's reliance on digital connectivity can actually weaken a once-solid social fabric.[41] This replacement of authentic, real-world connections with connections based in superficial digital realms can, arguably, compromise a community's resilience. If technology is necessary in your creative work, ensure it plays a **supporting role** and never replaces face-to-face human connection.

> Consider the **supporting role** that technology played during the COVID-19 pandemic, but only insofar as it supplemented the existing deep social relationships and cooperative systems we had previously established.

Show up and share your skills

Social justice and effective advocacy aren't solo sports. Being active community members and showing up both online and in person to contribute to the causes we're passionate about is critical to our roles as conscious creatives. Whether we're pulled to climate change, disability justice, mental health, racial justice, gender equity, animal rights, queer and trans issues, wealth distribution, decoloniality, labour justice, or something else entirely, let's do our part by working to enhance communication, organizing workshops, or participating in advocacy and resistance efforts whether on the frontlines or behind the scenes. Whatever our cause, let's commit to showing up and sharing our skills.

Chapter
Four
Environmental
Actions

Solidify your stance on eco-issues

I've said it before and I'll say it again: Defining our position is absolutely essential to an ethical practice. As creatives who are mindful of **climate impact** and the ecosystems we affect, we must educate ourselves on, and decide where we draw the line on, key topics.

> **Research indicates that fossil fuel burning is the most significant contributor to climate change. It has been said that we (well, big business, since one hundred corporations are responsible for 71 percent of greenhouse emissions, according to one study[1]) must cut usage by 45 percent in approximately a decade in order to mitigate significant climate collapse. Certainly corporations account for much of the problem, but we can all do our part by mitigating our own impact, voting with our dollars, and advocating for safer practices that protect the earth, animals, and ourselves.**

What do we consider to be clean energy? How can we get involved in the politics of climate action? How do things like social justice and guaranteed basic income support the climate fight? What is our stance on animal welfare? Water conservation? A **circular economy**? Which materials do we consider to be ethical for use in our practice? What about the impact of companies in the dirtiest industries, such as oil and fashion? Who is mitigating those impacts successfully? How can we advocate for change?

Environmental Actions

145

> A **circular economy** aims to redesign the way our extract-create-waste economy functions by keeping materials in use, designing out pollution and waste, and regenerating natural ecosystems.

Once we've established where we stand, let's channel our inner Autumn Peltier or Greta Thunberg and speak up. Working in an office environment? When leaders and employees within an organization are vocal about their values as they relate to environmental issues, it has been proven to positively impact the success of a company's sustainability programs.[2]

Say goodbye to greenwashing

Greenwashing happens when we jump on an eco-is-trendy bandwagon and overstate the eco-friendliness of a product or service. In doing so, we dramatically *understate* the associated negative impacts. Buyer (and creative) beware. The marketplace is rife with misrepresented toxicity levels, false environmental performance facts, and overinflated (or all-out untrue) "all natural" claims.

It has been argued that without doing our due diligence in ensuring the accuracy of claims, we are complicit in the deception of our audiences.[3] It's critical, therefore, to investigate the products or services we are asked to promote. Let's ask the hard questions about things like GMOs and energy use, and whether products harbour chemicals that might be dangerous to the land, animals, or human health. Consider going even further to scrutinize a product's ingredients, the methods used for harvesting or extracting those materials, and the associated supply chain.[4]

So, what if we're asked to greenwash? We can push back and work hard not to misuse words like *organic* and *all natural*. We can do our best to avoid excessive use of the natural colour schemes and imagery that deceptively implies healthfulness and a thriving planet. We can use our creative prowess to do the job and get paid without misleading the public into believing that something is cleaner and safer than it actually is. Let's do what we can to *show the truth* and support consumers to make informed decisions about the impacts of what they buy.[5]

Assess project impact

Philosopher Tony Fry suggests that something must be destroyed in order to bring something new into existence.[6] Let's commit to consistently considering that which must be destroyed in order for us to create. We can start every project by asking ourselves: What are the impacts to our natural environment associated with this job? With the service or product itself? With my client or supplier? Research is everything. Some of nature's most damaging adversaries aren't so obvious—consider cheap T-shirts, online shopping, and tasty avocado toast.[7]

Further, creative work can be a messy venture, and excess waste can be a consequence. Responsible creatives (like us) familiarize ourselves with the rules and constraints of our local waste disposal, compost, and recycling initiatives so as to make informed choices about how to move things like creative tools, paper, and "disposable" products on to their next life. Locally sourced materials are often far less ecologically destructive than their internationally sourced counterparts. The reasons for this include a lowered reliance on air transportation and fossil fuels, a reduction in air pollution, the preservation of small farms and local manufacturers, and a reduction of our overall **carbon footprint**.

Awareness about the impact of our work will support consistent choices over the course of our careers to positively affect the planet and its creatures.

> Our **carbon footprint** is a way of talking about the total carbon emissions that we generate—individually or as a group or a company—with our actions, including the

way we travel, buy food, do laundry, use electronics, and more. A carbon footprint is usually calculated on a yearly basis. It has been suggested that reducing our individual footprints to 1.8 tons by 2050 is the best way to stabilize the climate.[8] The average American's footprint is currently 18.3 tons. In China, by comparison, the average individual footprint is about 8.2 tons.[9] We have some work to do, friends.

Recognize climate action as racial justice

Say it with me: Climate action is racial justice. Communities of colour are disproportionately denied access to safe, healthy environments. Black Americans are 54 percent more likely to be exposed to air pollution and three times more likely to die from lung disease than white Americans. Black communities are more likely to drink unhealthy water, live near toxic sites and landfills, and have elevated lead in their blood.[10] A recent study proved a consistent pattern of situating hazardous waste facilities and landfills in neighbourhoods where poor people and people of colour live.[11] The same is true for Indigenous Peoples in Canada. The long-term health of more than half of the First Nations in the country is dangerously affected by industrial pollution from contaminants like arsenic and mercury in the soil and waterways.[12] It behooves those of us developing the creative work that emotionally and strategically informs the public to use our skills to passionately advocate to end the ongoing violence of environmental racism. Let's commit to creating in ways that advocate for and activate the corporate and government decision makers among us to enact immediate change for those who are disproportionately bearing the burden of pollution.

Favour fair trade

When we choose clients or products with a Fairtrade certification,[13] we're connecting to practices that include environmental sustainability and empowering opportunities for marginalized stakeholders. The certification ensures fair, honest, and ethical approaches for the environment and humans alike. It is especially important if we are working with organizations whose businesses involve products often connected to problematic farming or labour practices, such as coffee, sugar, tea, flowers, cacao/chocolate, cotton, and bananas, to name a few. These industries can have devastating environmental and human impacts due to practices that destroy rainforests and reduce biodiversity, cause soil erosion or chemical contamination, or involve the use of slave and child labour. We can look for Fairtrade and B Corporation certifications to ensure we're working with ethical companies, and—when we're not—we can advocate for more responsible practices.

Make in moderation

As we might expect, environmentally mindful creation is a less-is-more affair. We can start to live these values by lowering our resource consumption and mitigating our impact. Look for environmental certifications like Forest Stewardship Certified (FSC) paper and products that use biodegradable and compostable materials.[14] Seek out labels that indicate reduced carbon impact, no ozone-depleting substances, recycled and recyclable materials, and chlorine-free production. Upcycle and reuse materials whenever possible. Get familiar with organizations like **Canopy** and certifications like Energy Star, EcoLogo, and Rainforest Alliance Certified.[15]

To create in moderation means thinking smaller, creating with fewer superfluous elements, and always using materials that break down over time. It means aiming to make our creations last and avoiding planned obsolescence at all costs. Creativity can be maximized by producing within constraints, such as using only repurposed and local materials or avoiding excess embellishment.

> **Canopy** is an awesome organization that supports creative organizations in publishing, fashion, and beyond to reshape their purchasing practices in ways that protect and conserve forests and ecosystems. They may be best known for "greening" a very famous series of books about a child wizard that our kid is obsessed with.

Consume climate content

With thousands of folks warning us that "our house is on fire," there is no shortage of educational media on the topic of climate change and environmental degradation. We might consider reading *This Changes Everything* by Naomi Klein to get a grasp on the connection between capitalism and the climate; we can watch or read *Merchants of Doubt*, which exposes how a small group of scientists obscured evidence of climate change; *The Sixth Extinction* by Elizabeth Kobert details our possible descent toward mass extinction; *Heat* by George Monbiot investigates the steps we might take to fight back against global warming; and *Climate Change* by Dr. Joseph Romm outlines how the climate crisis could affect our lives. Consider, as well, listening to a climate podcast like *Warm Regards* by Jacquelyn Gill or BBC's *Costing the Earth*.

Consume climate content with a caveat: It's an intense topic, so take care of yourself first. If the content is causing too much anxiety or proving to feel hopeless instead of help-ful, then take a break, do something kind for yourself (forest bathing, anyone?), and take some space. We are of no help to the climate or each other in a state of panic or apathy.

Champion nature's rights

Across the world and under most legal systems, nature is considered property with no rights of its own.[16] As such, nature's treatment—and the choice to destroy or compromise its ecosystems—is entirely up to whomever owns that property. To champion the rights of the natural world is to unlearn these philosophies that dominate Western society and consider nature as an independent entity with the right to flourish.[17] This radical shift to our dominant beliefs is one that many argue is critical if we are to have any chance against climate change. We can educate ourselves on the history of this thinking by working toward an understanding of Indigenous land knowledge, the U.N.'s World Charter for Nature and its Harmony with Nature programme, and the Rights of Nature movement.[18]

Offset your carbon use

Carbon offsetting is a means of allowing individuals and companies to mitigate the impact of their greenhouse gas emissions, or carbon footprints.[19] However, it is only a small, incremental measure to be implemented while we work on larger goals and it is generally regarded as insufficient to replace larger systemic solutions like radically cutting emissions by terminating our use of fossil fuels entirely.

So, how does it work? Let's say we have an opportunity to fly from Toronto to Mexico City for a creative conference. Start with the questions: Do I really need this flight? Can I do this in a way that is more energy efficient? Are there greener travel alternatives? Can I pull a Greta and take a low-emission boat instead?

If we decide the conference is essential and there is no viable travel alternative, then carbon offsetting can allow us to effectively neutralize the greenhouse gases associated with our travel plans, as we will reduce our usage somewhere else instead.[20] We can take advantage of **carbon offsetting programs** that help us to invest in renewable energy projects when we feel it's necessary to offset our actions.

> A quick Google (or DuckDuckGo, the search engine that doesn't track users) of "top **carbon offset providers** in [my country]" will connect you with services to support an offsetting endeavour.

Don't just sustain — regenerate

Regenerative design takes sustainability one step further and aims to build systems that naturally regenerate lost resources back into existence. This involves deep consideration of the ways in which humans and the environment coexist.

Consider the popular example of "for every purchase you make, we'll plant a tree!" This is a restorative (not regenerative) measure that can certainly have its benefits, but developing naturally regenerating ecosystems (as in permaculture) restores a deeper level of resilience. We can consider regenerative methods when pitching eco-friendly partnerships to clients and collaborators, or aim to get involved in regeneration efforts outside of office hours.

Work from home

Beyond the benefits of increased productivity and providing our own childcare (whether for littles of the fur, plant, or human variety), working from home reduces emissions and positively impacts public health and the climate by taking vehicles off the road on daily commutes. Studies suggest that the American workforce avoids somewhere around 2.7 billion trips per year by working remotely. That equals a savings of thirty million metric tonnes of CO_2e per year.[21] Not only is remote work proven to be better on the environment, but it is shown to increase productivity, result in more inclusive hiring, keep employees healthy (turns out 60 percent of workers still go to the office when they're sick),[22] and offer a more balanced work-life, which improves mental health. We can consider all of that justification enough to stay in our PJs (at least on the bottom) and video call in to that next meeting. And when we go into the office? Let's consider taking transit, rolling, walking, or cycling, if possible.

Choose your clients wisely

Investigating the impact of our clients in order to ensure we're not complicit in environmentally destructive practices is a critical step to becoming a conscious creative. Let's aim to choose our clients wisely—with the caveat we discussed earlier in the book. Some people believe that the best way to effect change in an ethically questionable organization is to subvert from within. Ask: Can I add value to a business whose practices are currently less than ideal?

Enacting change is a worthy uphill climb, but it is also perfectly acceptable to decline working for a client whose values don't align with our own. If we have strong feelings about industries like oil, fashion, mining, development, or industrial agriculture, we can consider conjuring our inner activist. Let's stay current on our knowledge about the issues associated with certain industries, and speak out and educate our colleagues. We can channel our energy into partnerships with organizations that share our values and those that support the goals we want to achieve.

Choose your suppliers wisely

Being mindful about our impact means considering the practices of the entire network of people and organizations with whom we work. Aim to understand a partner's approach to things like energy conservation, manufacturing, and production processes.

Suppliers with a commitment to environmental stewardship typically make it a point to market themselves as such, but let's not allow that to dissuade us from doing our due diligence. We can start by asking potential partners about recycled content, emissions and energy efficiency, attempts to produce products with fewer toxins, product life-cycles, and approaches to disposal and reuse. We can share resources, talk to other creatives who share our penchant for responsible work, and check out government websites that list support for sustainable sourcing and purchasing.

Start an eco-initiative

We know this by now: Companies increasingly understand the value of operating in ways that mitigate negative environmental impact. Unfortunately, however, those companies don't always have resources at the ready to spearhead their initiatives. So, let's put on our leadership pants (they can fit over our generosity pants), pitch an idea to the powers that be, and initiate programs with climate action, environmental protection, and regeneration at their core.

And if the company doesn't buy our idea? We can consider starting an initiative within our local community. We might organize folks to start upcycling otherwise landfill-bound products or design communications that promote low-waste lifestyles and empower consumers to buy chemical-free. We can support "binners" in our neighbourhoods, who collect glass and cans for recycling; get involved in parks projects or community gardens; or become a member of our local **transition town**.[23] If we have a willingness to take a leadership or organizational role in advancing eco-initiatives, the list of opportunities is nearly endless.

> **Transition towns** are grassroots projects that intend to increase a community's self-sufficiency and reduce the harmful potential effects of peak oil, climate destruction, and economic instability. Check out **transitionnetwork.org.**

Assess your personal impact

It's a fact that approximately 20 percent of people (mostly in wealthy countries like Canada and the U.S.) consume in excess of 80 percent of the world's natural resources.[24] While we work toward and advocate for globally implemented systemic change, let's start to put a dent in that number by addressing our individual practices as a starting point.

Some folks practice meatless Mondays or vegan Thursdays to consider animal welfare, take positive steps to address climate change, and improve their health. Others aim to alter their idea of entertainment in a way that fosters more experience and less shopping and consumption.

Making a shift in our overall impact doesn't have to involve a radical lifestyle overhaul. Start small. Drive a little less. Turn off the lights. Take a shorter shower. Stop using single-use plastics. Make clothes last a bit longer. Buy organic and fair trade. We can stay connected to impact-related research and continually learn how to reduce our own footprint.[25] Most importantly, let's aim for balance above all; decisions that border on ascetic won't be conducive to long-term, sustainable change.

Detox from dirty data

Spread the word: The seemingly infinite capacity of that nebulous data "cloud" is in fact a series of big, metal data farms emitting greenhouse gases all over the world. Studies show that communication technologies may account for approximately 3.5 percent of global emissions in 2020. This means our connected devices are effectively dirtier than both aviation and shipping combined.[26] As companies work to make the switch toward renewable energy (currently 80 percent of our power still comes from fossil fuels), we can do our part by being smart about data use.

We can start by reminding our colleagues and organizations that paperless is not necessarily more eco-friendly. Consider sending less email. Store only the data that is absolutely needed. Use green hosting solutions that tout renewable energy resources. Disconnect devices and indulge in a digital detox where possible. Our brains will thank us too.[27]

Make at a local scale

We should aim to create small-scale interventions that are specific to the needs of, and run by, local communities. Our networks will be tighter, our projects will feel manageable, we'll use fewer resources, the communities we're creating with will be better represented, and the voices of all constituents will be heard. Think big and make small.

Expand your definition of social

Let's take a cue from social innovation movements and look at what they really mean by their intention of working to meet social goals. We can start by asking who "social" really includes. Are we only supporting humans, or should we expand that definition? The research conducted by the Emily Carr University DESIS (Design for Social Innovation and Sustainability) lab in Vancouver, Canada, for example, aims to include social relations with *more than* humans. The team looks at the integrated relationships between animals, the environment, and people to support the development of more holistic project priorities that benefit the entire natural world.[28]

Recombine existing assets

All too often, innovation is synonymous with the sort of newness that pristine, fresh-out-of-the-box technology has. In the world of conscious creativity, however, where the aim is to lower resource intensity, we seek to find ways to innovate without increasing consumer volume. Our greatest tool for achieving this is to recombine existing assets wherever possible. Each year, the World Economic Forum hosts a celebration of creativity called "The Circulars" that awards people making innovative contributions to the circular economy—many of whom develop impressive and environmentally impactful projects with existing assets.[29] Close the Loop, an Australian Company, discovered how to use old printer cartridges and soft plastics to make roads; Enerkem creates biofuel out of trash that has resulted in at least one Canadian city now using 90 percent of all its waste; and Hyla Mobile has managed to repurpose and reuse over fifty million discarded mobile devices.[30]

Create to reduce consumption

This challenging action falls at the end of the list for a reason: Too often, our everyday creative work involves an inevitable end-goal of driving consumption. Let's attempt to subvert that. One proven way to reduce our audience's desire to buy more stuff is to create in such a way that fosters conviviality and discourages competitive relations between people that can cause envy and a desire to "keep up."[31] We might consider nodding to thrifting or DIY culture in our work, reinforcing the freedom and lack of stress of owning less, or promoting alternative uses for disposable income like contributing to change-making organizations.

Let's make this a consideration when assessing the quality of the content we're creating and the subtle messages, visual or otherwise, that appear within our work. Studies have shown that competitive consumer behaviour is associated with an increase in mental health issues, and that there are significant social and environmental benefits to reducing consumption. We can dissuade our audience from mindless buying by instead encouraging behaviours that are core to human well-being, like harmony with nature, fun and leisure, healthfulness, and spending quality time with those we love.[32]

"Making a shift in our overall impact doesn't have to involve a radical lifestyle overhaul. Start small."

Conclusion

Intentions matter.

We made it to the end of this book because we share an intention to use our careers and our talents to incrementally improve the world where we can. That awareness and purpose, by my way of thinking, means we can unquestionably consider ourselves to be conscious creatives.

This book is a modest contribution to an evolving world where ethical pursuits are of increasing importance in the face of today's most pressing social, political, economic, and climate-related issues.

Now it's time for us to act.

There will be actions we choose to implement today, and there will be those which resonate but may not feel immediately possible. Both are important. We can act now while also collecting a set of aspirational goals to fuel the future of our practice and develop a unique, values-based roadmap for our careers. Whether we continue to work in a commercial industry, making small compromises while advocating for ethical action where possible, or forsake it altogether to pursue creating for the greater good full-time, the point is that we're doing *something*.

I believe that every action, regardless of size, has the capacity to have meaningful, multi-layered impact because I have a great deal of belief in our collective power. May we continue to act and coax the creative industries until they evolve into leading models of ethical practice.

And as for me?

Am I ready to acquiesce and re-enter the advertising industry? Am I ready to accept my role within a troublesome and sophisticated system of persuasion and consumption? Am I prepared to face the realities of aggressive workplaces, ableism, discrimination, questionable client practices, and unreasonable beauty standards? Do I miss the people? The passion? The openness to outrageously creative solutions and the big budgets that enable them? The potential within those budgets to enact change on a really significant scale?

Full disclosure: I'm still not sure.

What I am certain of is that in my freelance creative direction and writing career, I am prepared to address the issues that I face head-on. I am prepared to have a voice, to get involved, and to support others to work in ways that encourage safe, supportive, and sustainable practices. I am prepared to choose my clients and agencies wisely and to subvert from within when I, inevitably, find myself in ethically questionable settings.

I will commit to mindful action. I will never write or accept a brief without asking if something bigger—something more meaningful—can be achieved. I will remember that ethics are a daily practice. I will set achievable goals. Most importantly, I have learned to find peace and purpose in my conscious creativity. I am committed to acting as ethically as I can while accepting my compulsory participation in a problematic capitalist paradigm. Both things can coexist. At times they will conflict with each other, and, for now, I am okay with that.

What really matters is an ongoing practice of intentional, mindful, and responsible action.

And that can happen anywhere.

Thought of an action that wasn't covered in the book? Feelings coming up around the content you just read? Have some feedback for me? Tweet **@kelly_small** and let's have a conversation.

Gratitude

I wish I could go back in time and let existential crisis me know that everything's going to be okay. I would tell me that everything feels wrong for a reason. That my instincts are right. That dismantling old values, priorities, and ideas about what success means is tough, but that doing so creates space for new relationships and learning from incredible, conscious folks with shared sensibilities. I would tell me that this wild ride culminates in a project to be proud of and one inspired and supported by amazing people whose contributions I won't be able to even begin to share my gratitude for.

But I'll try.

First, my wife, Dahlia. You were holding my hand at the moment this idea was conceived and you haven't let go. This project could never have happened without inspiration from your magical way in the world, your enthusiastic support, and your exquisite love. This story would have turned out very differently had you not walked into my life. Thank you, my love.

To Philip Powell, my first creative hero. The person who saw a spark of something early in my career and took a chance on me. I wouldn't be where I am if it wasn't for your guidance, encouragement, and above all friendship. You were the definition of a conscious creative. You are forever missed, and I hope you're proud.

I am grateful to the conscious, supportive, and inspiring grad studies faculty at Emily Carr University:

Katherine Gillieson, Craig Badke, Louise St. Pierre, Garnet Hertz, Helene Day Fraser, Rita Wong, and Gillian Russell. I am grateful for the safe, intersectional, and queer-positive space the ECU community of staff, faculty, and students afforded me as I worked to redefine myself as a creative and rethink my approach to practice. Thank you as well to all of my amazing MDes colleagues and friends from the industry who generously participated in my graduate research.

Gratitude to the entire team of conscious creatives at House of Anansi Press for believing in this project and committing to responsible making, every time. To the kind and formidable Semareh Al-Hillal, thank you for being so generous with your time and support, for seeing something in that early manuscript, and for being a friend. Likewise, to my intensely talented editor Michelle MacAleese. Thank you for championing *The Conscious Creative* with such passion and enthusiasm. We've shared a vision for this project from day one and I am grateful to have the best of the best on my team. I knew we were meant to be when, in our first meeting, you handed me a mug that said, "First coffee, then the patriarchy." Every member of the Anansi team has been a dream to work with. Special thanks to the talented *Conscious Creative* dream team that includes Alysia Shewchuk, Maria Golikova, Ricky Lima, Laura Brady, Karen Brochu, Laura Chapnick, and Curtis Samuel.

And, of course, my deepest gratitude to my family and friends for getting me here: My sweet Evan, who, upon learning about this book, said, "Kelly's going to be famous!" (May this bubble never burst.) My mom, for believing in me and for your endless love and support. Myrna, I am so grateful for your invaluable feedback on early edits; your belief in the project has been so meaningful. Plants. I couldn't have done it without your encouragement and limitless patience for my incessant "which version do you like best?" texts. Dad, Jackie, Michael, and Sam, thank you for your support, for being proud of me, and for seeing me through this process. You'll never know how much it means. Likewise, to Nicole, Noodies, Terra, Robin, Shruti, Niamh, Donna, Vickie, Lana, and everyone else who has supported me in this project. Thank you.

A final shout-out to everybody whose path I've crossed in the creative industries. Thank you for joining me on this adventure and for your desire to use your talent to create in ways that leave things a little better than we found them. I wish you a kind, humane, and peaceful career that allows you to achieve way more than what capitalism tells you is valuable.

I can't end this without thanking my creative power trifecta®: Roxane Gay, Hannah Gadsby, and Maria Bamford. I've never been one for idolatry, but the masterful, deeply vulnerable, nothing-short-of-transformative work each of you do is as close to a religious experience as I'm ever going to get. Thank you for showing me that achievement while remaining true to oneself isn't just possible, it's the way.

Notes

Introduction

1. Max Nathan, Tom Kemeny, and Andy Pratt, "Creative Economy Employment in the U.S., Canada and the U.K.," *Nesta Reports*, March 23, 2016, nesta.org.uk/report/creative-economy-employment-in-the-us-canada-and-the-uk/.

2. Stuart Walker, *Designing Sustainability: Making Radical Changes in a Material World* (Milton Park, U.K.: Routledge, 2014), 42.

3. Melody Wilding, "The Japanese Concept 'Ikigai' Is a Formula for Happiness and Meaning," Better Humans section, Medium, November 30, 2017, medium.com/better-humans/the-japanese-concept-ikigai-is-a-formula-for-happiness-and-meaning-8e497e5afa99.

4. John Howkins, *The Creative Economy: How People Make Money from Ideas* (London: Penguin Random House U.K., 2013).

5. Lucienne Roberts, *Good: An Introduction to Ethics in Graphic Design* (Lausanne, Switzerland: AVA Publishing, 2006), 28.

6. Eileen M. Kane, "Fish Tales," Ethics in Graphic Design, June 14, 2011, ethicsingraphicdesign.org/fish-tales/.

7. Ken Garland, *First Things First* (London: Ken Garland/Goodwin Press, 1964).

8. René Spitz, "Design Is Not a Science: Otl Aicher's Constitutional Putsch at the HfG Ulm and His Credo for the Social Responsibility of Designers," *Design Issues* 31, no. 1 (Winter 2015): 7–17.

9. Steven Heller and Véronique Vienne, eds., *Citizen Designer: Perspectives on Design Responsibility* (New York: Allworth Press, 2003), 103.

10. John Emerson, "100+ Years of Manifestos," *Backspace* (blog), March 18, 2019, backspace.com/notes/2009/07/design-manifestos.php; Nguyet Vuong, "Milton Glaser's A Designer's the Road to Hell," *New Way Design* (blog), January 23, 2016, newwaydesign.com/milton-glasers-a-

designers-the-road-to-hell/; Jonathan Barnbrook et al., "First Things First Manifesto 2000," *Eye* magazine (Autumn 1999), eyemagazine.com/feature/article/first-things-first-manifesto-2000.

11. Heller and Vienne, eds., *Citizen Designer*, 103.

12. Majid H. Jafar, "What's Wrong with Capitalism?," in *Performance and Progress*, ed. Subramanian Rangan (Oxford: Oxford University Press, 2015), 11–27, oxfordscholarship.com/view/10.1093/acprof:oso/9780198744283.001.0001/acprof-9780198744283-chapter-2.

13. The 3% Movement, 3percentmovement.com.

14. Eileen M. Kane, "Summary," *Ethics of Design* (blog), April 19, 2013, ethicsofdesign.wordpress.com/summary; Noah Scalin and Michelle Taute, *The Design Activist's Handbook: How to Change the World (Or at Least Your Part of It) with Socially Conscious Design* (Cincinnati, OH: HOW Books, 2012), 19.

15. *Merriam-Webster*, s.v. "ethic *(n.)*," merriam-webster.com/dictionary/ethic.

16. *Oxford U.S. Dictionary*, s.v. "ethical *(adj.)*," en.oxforddictionaries.com/definition/us/ethical.

17. Katharine Schwab, "Design Is Inherently an Unethical Industry," *Fast Company*, August 30, 2017, fastcompany.com/90138470/Design-is-inherently-an-Unethical-industry; Sean Illing, Kurt Wagner, and Karen Turner, "Has Facebook Been Good for the World?," *Vox*, February 4, 2019, vox.com/technology/2019/2/4/18205138/facebook-15-anniversary-social-network-founded-date-2004.

18. Tony Fry, *Design Futuring: Sustainability, Ethics and New Practice* (Oxford: Berg, 2009), 80.

19. Fry, *Design Futuring*, 4.

20. Neil Postman, "Five Things We Need to Know about Technological Change," speech, March 28, 1998, Denver, CO, web.cs.ucdavis.edu/~rogaway/classes/188/materials/postman.pdf; Langdon Winner, "Technologies as Forms of Life," *Ethics and Emerging Technologies*, ed. R. L. Sandler (London: Palgrave Macmillan, 2014), 48–60; Andrew Feenberg, "Ten Paradoxes of Technology," *Techné: Research in Philosophy and Technology* 14, no. 1 (Winter 2010): 3–15.

21. Bruno Latour, "Love Your Monsters: Why We Must Care for Our Technologies as We Do Our Children," *The Breakthrough*, no. 2 (Fall 2011), thebreakthrough.org/journal/issue-2/love-your-monsters.

22. "Distinguish Yourself as a Certified RGD," RGD (Association of Registered Graphic Designers), updated January 2020, rgd.ca/rgd-certification/certification; "CGD™ Certification," Graphic Designers of Canada, gdc.design/cgd-certification/about.

23. Samantha Dempsey and Ciara Taylor, "Explore where the Designer's Oath Has Been!" Designer's Oath, last modified 2016, designersoath.com.

24. Roberts, *Good*, 36.

25. SparkNotes editors, "Nicomachean Ethics: Books I to IV," SparkNotes, accessed December 2, 2019, sparknotes.com/philosophy/aristotle/section8/.

26. Roberts, *Good*, 192.

27. Judith Samuelson and Americus Reed, "When Do Consumer Boycotts Work?," The Opinion Pages, *The New York Times*, February 7, 2017, nytimes.com/roomfordebate/2017/02/07/when-do-consumer-boycotts-work.

28. Roberts, *Good*, 127.

29. Eileen M. Kane, *Ethics: A Graphic Designer's Field Guide* (New York: Campbell Hall Press, 2010).

30. David Berman, *Do Good Design: How Design Can Change the World* (Berkeley, CA: New Riders, 2009), 1.

31. Clive Dilnot, "The Artificial and What It Opens Toward," in *Design and the Question of History*, co-authored with Tony Fry and Susan Stewart (New York: Bloomsbury Academic, 2015), 165–203.

32. TIME'S UP Advertising, "We're making gender equality the new normal," TIME'S UP Foundation, timesupadvertising.com.

33. Me Too Movement, metoomvmt.org.

34. Depatriarchise Design, depatriarchisedesign.com.

35. Decolonising Design, decolonisingdesign.com.

36. "Canadian Creative Industries Code of Conduct," Read the Code, readthecode.ca.

37. "Let's Make the Industry 50/50 Initiative," 50/50 Initiative, ADC, 5050initiative.org.

38. The 3% Movement, 3percentmovement.com.

39. "So(cial) Good Design Awards," RGD, rgd.ca/2015/03/02/social-good-design-awards-returns-in-2018.php; "Social Impact Media Awards," SIMA, simaawards.org/sima-awards-competition/; "The Fashion Impact Award," CAFA Awards, cafawards.ca/the-fashion-impact-award/; "AZ Social Good Awards," *Azure Magazine*, awards.azuremagazine.com/details/.

40. "Cannes Lions Awards — Good," Cannes Lions, canneslions.com/enter/awards.

41. "AIGA Design Census 2019," AIGA Design Census, designcensus.org/data/2019DesignCensus.pdf.

42. "RGD DesignThinkers 2018 Conference," DesignThinkers, designthinkers.com/; Ari Roth, "Ethical Design — 2018 SXSW Programming Trends," SXSW, January 26, 2018, sxsw.com/film/2018/ethical-design-2018-sxsw-programming-trends/.

43. Christopher Simmons, *Just Design: Socially Conscious Design for Critical Causes* (Cincinnati, OH: HOW Books, 2011), 4.

44. Fabricio Teixeira, "Diversity by Design: Our Role in Shaping a More Inclusive Industry," R/GA by Design section, Medium, June 1, 2017, rgabydesign.com/diversity-by-design-our-role-in-shaping-a-more-inclusive-industry-4efccd99e1c9; Bronwen Rees, "Diversity and Design: How We Can Shape a More Inclusive Industry?," UX Planet section, Medium, September 3, 2017, uxplanet.org/Diversity-and-design-how-we-can-shape-a-more-inclusive-industry-3b129999962e; Laura Snoad, "How to Encourage Diversity in the Design Industry," *Creative Bloq*, March 8, 2018, creativebloq.com/features/how-to-encourage-diversity-in-the-design-industry; Khoi Vinh, "Creative Careers Elude People of Color," Ideas section, *Quartz*, March 9, 2018, qz.com/1216574/creative-careers-elude-people-of-color/.

45. "About Us," Center for Humane Technology, humanetech.com/about-us/.

46. "DESIS Network," Design for Social Innovation and Sustainability, desisnetwork.org.

47. Andrew Kragie, "Vision without Execution Is Just a Hallucination," commencement address, in *Duke Today*, May 10, 2015, today.duke.edu/2015/05/kragie.

48. Robert L. Peters, "Design is the application of intent…," Twitter, quoted in *Quotes on Design*, quotesondesign.com/robert-l-peters/.

Chapter 1: Personal Actions

1. Roberts, *Good*, 192.

2. "Sustainable Development Goals," UN Sustainable Development Goals Knowledge Platform, sustainabledevelopment.un.org/?menu=1300.

3. "The Sustainable Development Goals," Global Compact Network Canada, globalcompact.ca/sustainable-development-goals/.

4. Kimberlé Crenshaw, "Demarginalizing the Intersection of Race and Sex: A Black Feminist Critique of Antidiscrimination Doctrine, Feminist Theory, and Antiracist Politics," in *University of Chicago Legal Forum*: 1 (1989), Article 8. chicagounbound.uchicago.edu/uclf/vol1989/iss1/8.

5. "The Spoon Theory," Christine Miserandino, 2003, butyoudontlooksick.com/the_spoon_theory.

6. "Social Justice Vocabulary," SOJI Education, The ARC Foundation, bc.sogieducation.org/social-justice-vocabulary/.

7. David Robert Grimes, "Echo Chambers Are Dangerous—We Must Try to Break Free of Our Online Bubbles," Note and Theories, *The Guardian*, December 4, 2017, theguardian.com/science/blog/2017/dec/04/echo-chambers-are-dangerous-we-must-try-to-break-free-of-our-online-bubbles.

8. Gwen Moran, "Are Microaggressions Trashing Your Company's Productivity?," *Fast Company*, September 27, 2018, fastcompany.com/90236557/are-microaggressions-trashing-your-companys-productivity.

9. Depatriarchise Design, depatriarchisedesign.com.

10. Design Justice Network, designjustice.org.

11. "Editorial Statement," Decolonising Design, updated November 15, 2017, decolonisingdesign.com/statements/2016/editorial/.

12. Heller and Vienne, eds., *Citizen Designer*, 192.

13. "In Apparel, It's Fast Fashion Versus Sustainability," *Lifestyle Monitor*, Cotton Incorporated, March 9, 2018. lifestylemonitor.cottoninc.com/in-apparel-its-fast-fashion-versus-sustainability/.

14. Adam Vaughan, "How Viral Cat Videos Are Warming the Planet," *The Guardian*, September 25, 2015, theguardian.com/environment/2015/

sep/25/server-data-centre-emissions-air-travel-web-google-facebook-greenhouse-gas.

15. Noah Scalin and Michelle Taute, *The Design Activist's Handbook: How to Change the World (Or at Least Your Part of It) with Socially Conscious Design* (Cincinnati, OH: HOW Books, 2012), 24.

16. Aaron Weyenberg, "The Ethics of Good Design: A Principle for the Connected Age," The Startup section, Medium, November 21, 2016, medium.com/swlh/dieter-rams-ten-principles-for-good-design-the-1st-amendment-4e73111a18e4; "10 of the Best Design Philosophies of All Time," Proto.io, last modified August 7, 2015, blog.proto.io/10-of-the-best-design-philosophies-of-all-time/; Katherine Schwab, "8 Design Principles to Live And Die By, According to Facebook, IBM, Pentagram, and More," *Fast Company*, September 26, 2017, fastcompany.com/90143505/8-design-principles-to-live-and-die-by-according-to-facebook-ibm-pentagram-and-more.

17. Author interview with Vivianne Castillo. October 30, 2019.

18. Brené Brown, *Rising Strong: How the Ability to Reset Transforms the Way We Live, Love, Parent, and Lead* (New York: Spiegel & Grau, 2017).

19. Alain Giguère, "44% of Canadians Are Socially Responsible Consumers," On My Radar This Week, *CROP* (blog), July 7, 2017, crop.ca/en/blog/2017/190/.

20. Heller and Vienne, eds., *Citizen Designer*, 227.

21. Scalin and Taute, *The Design Activist's Handbook*, 127.

22. "Social Impact Statistics You Should Know (2018)," Engage for Good, (2018). engageforgood.com/stats/.

23. Virginia Tassinari, "DESIS Philosophy Talks," *DESIS Philosophy Talks* (blog), desis-philosophytalks.org.

24. Scalin and Taute, *The Design Activist's Handbook*, 85, 96.

25. Heller and Vienne, eds., *Citizen Designer*, 187.

26. Deloitte, *The Deloitte Millennial Survey 2018*, August 23, 2018, deloitte.com/global/en/pages/about-deloitte/articles/millennialsurvey.html; Patrick Cook-Deegan and Kendall Cotton Bronk, "Want a Purpose-Driven Business? Know the Difference between Mission and Purpose," *Fast Company*, February 4, 2018, fastcompany.com/40552232/want-a-purpose-driven-business-know-the-difference-between-mission-and-purpose.

27. Author interview with Ailsa M. Blair. November 8, 2019.

28. Libby MacCarthy, "New Report Reveals 86% of U.S. Consumers Expect Companies to Act on Social, Environmental Issues," Sustainable Brands, May 18, 2017, sustainablebrands.com/news_and_views/ marketing_comms/libby_maccarthy/new_report_reveals_86_Americans_ expect_companies_take.

29. Roberts, *Good*, 65.

30. Virginia Tassinari, "DESIS Philosophy Talks" ; "DESIS Labs," DESIS Network (2016); desisnetwork.org/labs/; "We Are the Social Innovation Exchange," Social Innovation Exchange, socialinnovationexchange.org.

31. "Homepage," Participedia, participedia.net; "About," CitizenLab, citizenlab.co/about; "Homepage," Plume Labs, plumelabs.com/en/; "Profile," MASS LBP, masslbp.com/profile.

32. Roberts, *Good*, 65.

33. Ezio Manzini, *Design, When Everybody Designs: An Introduction to Design for Social Innovation* (Cambridge, MA: The MIT Press, 2015), 33.

34. Scalin and Taute, *The Design Activist's Handbook*, 24.

Chapter 2: Economic Actions

1. *Merriam-Webster*, s.v. "capitalism (*n.*)," merriam-webster.com/dictionary/ capitalism.

2. Jafar, "What's Wrong with Capitalism?" 11–27; Naomi Klein, "Capitalism Killed Our Climate Momentum, Not Human Nature," The Intercept, August 3, 2018, theintercept.com/2018/08/03/climate-change-new-york-times-magazine; Naomi Klein, *This Changes Everything: Capitalism vs. the Climate* (Toronto, ON: Vintage Canada, 2015).

3. Deloitte, *The Deloitte Millennial Survey 2018*.

4. "Report: Social Purpose Now a Key Driver in Canadians' Purchasing Decisions," Sustainable Brands, April 30, 2018, sustainablebrands.com/ news_and_views/business_case/sustainable_brands/Report_social_ purpose_now_key_driver_canadians_purch.

5. Emily Antoniadi, "Purpose Eh? How Canada Can Lead the Way," Kin&Co, April 19, 2018, kinandco.com/purpose-eh-how-canada-can-lead-the-way/; Adam Butler, "Do Customers Really Care about Your Environmental Impact?," *Forbes*, November 21, 2018, forbes.com/sites/

forbesnycouncil/2018/11/21/do-customers-really-care-about-your-environmental-impact/#57c3946f240d.

6. "No Spec," RGD, rgd.ca/resources/no-spec.

7. "Ico-D Stands against Crowd-Sourced Competition for the Tokyo Olympics 2020 Logo," International Council of Design, February 11, 2016, ico-d.org/2016/02/11/tokyo-logo-story.php; "No Spec," RGD; "About No!Spec," No!Spec (website), nospec.com.

8. "Design for Good," AIGA: The Professional Association for Design, aiga.org/design-for-good; "So(cial) Good Design Awards," RGD.

9. Scalin and Taute, *The Design Activist's Handbook*, 127.

10. 10. Elizabeth Warren, "Companies Shouldn't Be Accountable Only to Shareholders," Opinion, *The Wall Street Journal*, August 14, 2018, wsj.com/articles/companies-shouldnt-be-accountable-only-to-shareholders-1534287687.

11. CFA Institute, *2018 CFA Program Curriculum, Level II, Volume 3* (New Jersey: Wiley Global Finance, 2017).

12. Martin Zwilling, "8 Reasons Why Being Socially Responsible Is Good for Business," *Inc.com*, January 2, 2017, inc.com/martin-zwilling/8-reasons-why-being-socially-responsible-is-good-for-business.html; "Corporate Social Responsibility," Innovation, Science and Economic Development Canada, 2015, ic.gc.ca/eic/site/csr-rse.nsf/eng/h_rs00597.html.

13. "Home page," verynice (website), verynice.co.

14. "How to Give Half of Your Work Away for Free," verynice (website), givehalf.co.

15. "Charity Intelligence Canada," Charity Intelligence, charityintelligence.ca/; "Charity Navigator," Charity Navigator: Your Guide to Intelligent Giving, charitynavigator.org.

16. Sheena McKenzie, "Sexual Abuse 'Endemic' in International Aid Sector, Damning Report Finds," CNN, updated July 21, 2018, cnn.com/2018/07/30/uk/sexual-abuse-aid-sector-uk-report-intl/index.html.

17. "Is Your Money Paying for Animal Experiments?," Humane Charities Canada, humanecharities.ca/; "Protecting Pets, Wildlife, and Endangered Species," Animal Charities of America, animalcharitiesofamerica.org/home/.

18. Heller and Vienne, eds., *Citizen Designer*, 68.

19. Ibid.

20. CFA Institute, *2018 CFA Program Curriculum, Level II, Volume 3*, 45.

21. Berman, *Do Good Design*, 133.

22. Walker, *Designing Sustainability*, 91.

23. Clay Halton, "True Cost Economics," *Investopedia*, updated July 17, 2019, investopedia.com/terms/t/truecosteconomics.asp.

24. "Welcome to Bunz," Bunz, bunz.com.

25. Greig, Jonathan, "The 5 greenest tech companies in 2019," TechRepublic, techrepublic.com/article/the-5-greenest-tech-companies-in-2019/.

26. Zoë Schlanger, "Apple Wants to Try to 'Stop Mining the Earth Altogether' to Make Your iPhone," *Quartz*, April 20, 2017, qz.com/964862/apple-says-it-will-stop-using-rare-earth-minerals-to-make-iphones/.

27. "Home page," Creative Commons, creativecommons.org.

Chapter 3: Social Actions

1. Rikke Friis Dam and Yu Siang Teo, "How to Develop an Empathic Approach in Design Thinking," Interaction Design Foundation, interaction-design.org/literature/article/how-to-develop-an-empathic-approach-in-design-thinking.

2. Simmons, *Just Design*, 101.

3. Association of Registered Graphic Designers, *AccessAbility: A Practical Handbook on Accessible Web Design* (Toronto, ON: RGD, 2015), rgd.ca/resources/accessibility/access; "Disability Impacts All of Us," CDC, updated September 9, 2019, cdc.gov/ncbddd/disabilityandhealth/infographic-disability-impacts-all.html.

4. "Editorial Statement," Decolonising Design.

5. "Guide to Acknowledging First Peoples & Traditional Territory," Canadian Association of University Teachers, caut.ca/content/guide-acknowledging-first-peoples-traditional-territory.

6. Emily Moon, "The Research behind Getty Images' Ban on Photo Retouching for Body Shape," *Pacific Standard*, September 28, 2017, psmag.com/social-justice/the-research-behind-getty-images-ban-on-retouching.

7. Jamie Feldman, "Un-Retouched Ads Aren't a Huge Moneymaker, But Brands Don't Care," *HuffPost*, March 30, 2017, huffingtonpost.ca/entry/brands-no-photoshop_us_58dab41ce4b0546370629f88.

8. Wes Gay, "4 Reasons Why a Corporate Volunteer Program Is a Smart Investment," *Forbes*, November 14, 2016, forbes.com/sites/wesgay/2016/11/03/4-reasons-why-a-corporate-volunteer-program-is-a-smart-investment/#3906e8f93364.

9. Amy Adkins and Brandon Rigoni, "Paycheck or Purpose: What Drives Millennials?," Gallup, June 1, 2016, gallup.com/workplace/236453/paycheck-purpose-drives-millennials.aspx.

10. Roberts, *Good*, 133.

11. Olivia Solon, "Ex-Facebook President Sean Parker: Site Made to Exploit Human 'Vulnerability,'" *The Guardian*, November 9, 2017, theguardian.com/technology/2017/nov/09/facebook-sean-parker-vulnerability-brain-psychology.

12. Ian Leslie, "The Scientists Who Make Apps Addictive," *1843 Magazine*, October 20, 2016, 1843magazine.com/features/the-scientists-Who-make-apps-addictive; Simone Stolzoff, "The Formula for Phone Addiction Might Double as a Cure," *Wired*, February 1, 2018, wired.com/story/phone-addiction-formula/.

13. Jakob Nielsen, "Usability 101: Introduction to Usability," Nielson Norman Group, January 4, 2012, nngroup.com/articles/usability-101-introduction-to-usability/.

14. Shanghaiist.com, "Chinese Shoe Company Tricks People into Swiping Instagram Ad with Fake Strand of Hair," Shanghaiist section, Medium, December 15, 2017, medium.com/shanghaiist/chinese-shoe-company-tricks-people-into-swiping-instagram-ad-with-fake-strand-of-hair-54d8a2d8ec1d.

15. "Hall of Shame," Dark Patterns, darkpatterns.org/hall-of-shame.

16. UN General Assembly, *Convention on the Rights of Persons with Disabilities*, A/RES/61/106 (December 13, 2006), un.org/development/desa/disabilities/convention-on-the-rights-of-persons-with-disabilities.html.

17. Accessibility for Ontarians with Disabilities Act, 2005, S.O. 2005, c. 11, ontario.ca/laws/statute/05a11.

18. "How to Make Websites Accessible," Ontario government (website), ontario.ca/page/how-make-websites-accessible; "WCAG and

Government Web Standards in Canada," *Multiple Media* (blog), multiplemedia.com/en/blog/wcag-government-web-standards-in-canada.

19. "PIPEDA Fair Information Principles," Office of the Privacy Commissioner of Canada, priv.gc.ca/en/privacy-topics/privacy-laws-in-canada/the-personal-information-protection-and-electronic-documents-act-pipeda/p_principle/.

20. Tristan Harris, "How Technology Is Hijacking Your Mind— From a Magician and Google Design Ethicist," Thrive Global section, Medium, May 18, 2016, medium.com/thrive-global/how-Technology-hijacks-peoples-minds-from-a-magician-and-google-S-design-ethicist-56d62ef5edf3.

21. Sophie Weiner, "Applying the Addictive Psychology of Slot Machines to App Design," *Fast Company*, December 5, 2015, fastcompany.com/3046149/applying-the-addictive-psychology-of-slot-machines-to-app-design.

22. Danijela Maras, Martine F. Flament, Marisa Murray, Annick Buchholz, Katherine A. Henderson, Nicole Obeid, and Gary S. Goldfield, "Screen Time Is Associated with Depression and Anxiety in Canadian Youth," *Preventive Medicine* 73 (2015), 133–138; Lulu Garcia-Navarro, "The Risk of Teen Depression and Suicide Is Linked to Smartphone Use, Study Says," Mental Health section, NPR, December 17, 2017, npr.org/2017/12/17/571443683/the-call-in-teens-and-depression; Jean M. Twenge, Thomas E. Joiner, Megan L. Rogers, and Gabrielle N. Martin, "Increases in Depressive Symptoms, Suicide-Related Outcomes, and Suicide Rates among U.S. Adolescents after 2010 and Links to Increased New Media Screen Time," *Clinical Psychological Science* 6, no. 1 (January 2018), 3–17; Jean M. Twenge, "Have Smartphones Destroyed a Generation?," *The Atlantic*, September 2017, theatlantic.com/magazine/archive/2017/09/has-the-smartphone-destroyed-a-generation/534198/.

23. "About Us," Center for Humane Technology, humanetech.com/; "We Are a Catalyst and Connector for Tech Change," All Tech Is Human, alltechishuman.org.

24. Francis Lord, "Net Neutrality in Canada," *HillNotes* (blog), Canadian Library of Parliament, September 20, 2018, hillnotes.ca/2018/09/20/net-neutrality-in-canada/.

25. Ibid.

26. Mark Wilson, "What You're Getting Wrong about Inclusive Design," *Fast Company*, April 4, 2018, fastcompany.com/90166413/what-youre-getting-wrong-about-inclusive-design.

27. Heller and Vienne, eds., *Citizen Designer*, 100.

28. Matthew Hughes, "Study Shows We're Spending an Insane Amount of Time Online," The Next Web, January 30, 2019, thenextweb.com/tech/2019/01/31/study-shows-were-spending-an-insane-amount-of-time-online/; "The Ethical Digital Citizen," Study Hub, studyhub.fxplus.ac.uk/digital-me/ethical-digital-citizen; Rashmi Airan, "Are You Practicing Digital Ethical Citizenship?" *RASHMI* (blog), October 13, 2017, rashmiairan.com/ethical-digital-citizenship/.

29. Miriam M. Ahmed, "Minority Designers—Leading the Charge toward Responsible Design," in *Citizen Designer: Perspectives on Design Responsibility*, eds. Steven Heller and Véronique Vienne (New York: Allworth Press, 2003), 103–107, 203; Ben Paynter, "The Next Wave of Tech-for-Good Companies Are Being Built by Women and Minorities," *Fast Company*, April 10, 2018, fastcompany.com/40554684/the-next-wave-of-tech-for-good-companies-are-being-built-by-women-and-minorities.

30. "The State of Diversity and Funding in the Tech Nonprofit Sector," *Fast Forward* (blog), April 4, 2018, ffwd.org/blog/diversity-funding-tech-nonprofit-sector/.

31. "The Benefits of Co-operatives," Co-operatives U.K., updated October 16, 2017, uk.coop/about/benefits-co-operatives.

32. Steve Nguyen, "Creating an Ethical Organizational Culture," Workplace Psychology, February 14, 2011, workplacepsychology.net/2011/02/14/creating-an-ethical-organizational-culture/.

33. Heller and Vienne, eds., *Citizen Designer*, 91.

34. Simmons, *Just Design*, 13.

35. Andrew Shea, *Designing for Social Change: Strategies for Community-Based Graphic Design* (New York: Princeton Architectural Press, 2012), 97.

36. Anne Chick and Paul Micklethwaite, *Design for Sustainable Change: How Design and Designers Can Drive the Sustainability Agenda* (London: Bloomsbury Visual Arts, 2017).

37. Shea, *Designing for Social Change*, 83.

38. Ibid., 111.

39. The Design and Publishing Center, "Citizen Designer," DT&G Interviews, *DT&G* (blog), graphic-design.com/DTG/interviews/heller/.

40. "Election Design Tools and Resources," AIGA: The Professional Association for Design, aiga.org/aiga/content/why-design/design-for-democracy/election-design-tools-and-resources/.

41. Ezio Manzini, *Design, When Everybody Designs*, 33.

Chapter 4: Environmental Actions

1. Stuart Thomson, "So You Think Corporations Are Responsible for the World's Emissions? It's Not That Simple," *National Post*, October 14, 2018, nationalpost.com/news/politics/so-you-think-corporations-are-responsible-for-the-worlds-emissions-its-not-that-simple; Tess Riley, "Just 100 Companies Responsible for 71% of Global Emissions, Study Says," *The Guardian*, July 10, 2017, theguardian.com/sustainable-business/2017/jul/10/100-fossil-fuel-companies-investors-responsible-71-global-emissions-cdp-study-climate-change.

2. Walker, *Designing Sustainability*, 111.

3. Adrian Shaughnessy, *How to Be a Graphic Designer without Losing Your Soul* (New York: Princeton Architectural Press, 2010), 108–109.

4. "Think Dirty," Think Dirty® App, thinkdirtyapp.com/; "Green Choices — The green website for eco-living lifestyles," Green Choices, greenchoices.org.

5. "Sustainable Development Goals," Sustainable Development Goals Knowledge Platform, United Nations, sustainabledevelopment.un.org/?menu=1300.

6. Fry, *Design Futuring*, 4.

7. Naresh Ramchandani, "Nice Ad, Shame about the Planet," *Do the Green Thing* 10 (July 2018), dothegreenthing.com/issue/nice-ad-shame-about-the-planet/; Joanna Blythman, "Can Hipsters Stomach the Unpalatable Truth about Avocado Toast?," *The Guardian*, August 12, 2016, theguardian.com/commentisfree/2016/aug/12/hispters-Handle-unpalatable-truth-avocado-toast.

8. Deep Decarbonization Pathways Project, deepdecarbonization.org.

9. Renee Cho, "The 35 Easiest Ways to Reduce Your Carbon Footprint," Earth Institute, Columbia University, December 27, 2018, blogs. ei.columbia.edu/2018/12/27/35-ways-reduce-carbon-footprint/.

10. Zoë Schlanger, "Race Is the Biggest Indicator in the U.S. of Whether You Live Near Toxic Waste," *Quartz*, March 22, 2017, qz.com/939612/race-is-the-biggest-indicator-in-the-us-of-whether-you-live-near-toxic-waste/.

11. Brittany Whited, "With Environmental Rollbacks, Communities of Color Continue to Bear Disproportionate Pollution Burden," NYU School of Law—State Energy & Environmental Impact Centre, June 19, 2019, law. nyu.edu/centers/state-impact/press-publications/blog/environmental-justice-juneteenth-2019.

12. Hilary Beaumont, "More than half of First Nations communities in Canada are affected by industrial pollution," *Vice*, September 6, 2017, vice.com/en_ca/article/3kpj9k/more-than-half-of-first-nations-communities-in-canada-are-affected-by-industrial-pollution.

13. "Home page," Fairtrade Canada, fairtrade.ca.

14. "Forest Stewardship Council," FSC, fsc.org.

15. "ENERGY STAR for Products," Natural Resources Canada, nrcan.gc.ca/ energy/products/energystar/12519; "ECOLOGO® Certification Program," UL, industries.ul.com/environment/certificationvalidation-marks/ ecologo-product-certification; "Our Alliance Needs You," Rainforest Alliance, from rainforest-alliance.org/.

16. "What Is Rights of Nature?," Global Alliance for the Rights of Nature, therightsofnature.org/frequently-asked-questions/.

17. Tim Boucher, "World Charter for Nature (1982)," Medium, February 4, 2016, medium.com/@timboucher/world-charter-for-nature-1982-93cc3d41ff79.

18. UN General Assembly, *World Charter for Nature*, A/RES/37/7 (October 28, 1982), digitallibrary.un.org/record/39295?ln=en; "Programme," Harmony with Nature, United Nations, harmonywithnatureun.org/; "Champion the Rights of Nature," Community Environmental Legal Defense Fund, 2018, celdf.org/rights/rights-of-nature/.

19. "Carbon Offsets," David Suzuki Foundation, davidsuzuki.org/what-you-can-do/carbon-offsets/.

20. Madeleine Langechenier, "Carbon Offsetting: A Different Way to Reduce Greenhouse Gas Emissions," *Tree Canada* (blog), May 23,

2018, treecanada.ca/blog/carbon-offsetting-a-different-way-to-reduce-greenhouse-gas-emissions.

21. John Pflueger, Sarah Gibson, and Christian Normand, *The Sustainability Benefits of the Connected Workplace* (Round Rock, TX: DELL Inc., June 2016), i.dell.com/sites/doccontent/corporate/corp-comm/en/Documents/telecommute-study.pdf.

22. Conscious Media Company, "8 Reasons Companies Should Embrace Flexible Work Schedules," B The Change section, January 16, 2018, bthechange.com/8-reasons-companies-should-embrace-flexible-work-schedules-18f2befofc6.

23. "Transition Towns," Transition Network, transitionnetwork.org.

24. Philip White, Louise St. Pierre, and Steve Belletire, *Okala Practitioner: Integrating Ecological Design* (Phoenix, AZ: IDSA, 2013).

25. Chris Goodall, "How to Reduce Your Carbon Footprint," *The Guardian*, January 19, 2017, theguardian.com/environment/2017/jan/19/how-to-reduce-carbon-footprint.

26. "'Tsunami of Data' Could Consume One Fifth of Global Electricity by 2025," Climate Home News, *Guardian* Environment Network, December 11, 2017, theguardian.com/environment/2017/dec/11/tsunami-of-data-could-consume-fifth-global-electricity-by-2025.

27. Michaeleen Doucleff and Allison Aubrey, "Smartphone Detox: How to Power Down in a Wired World," NPR: Your Health, February 12, 2018, npr.org/sections/health-shots/2018/02/12/584389201/smartphone-detox-how-to-power-down-in-a-wired-world.

28. Louise St. Pierre, "DESIS: Design for Social Innovation and Sustainability," *Current* (blog), Emily Carr University of Art & Design, current.ecuad.ca/desis-br-design-for-social-innovation-and-sustainability.

29. "Homepage," The Circulars (website), thecirculars.org.

30. Alex Thornton, "These 11 companies are leading the way to a circular economy," World Economic Forum, February 26, 2019, weforum.org/agenda/2019/02/companies-leading-way-to-circular-economy/.

31. White, St. Pierre, and Belletire, *Okala Practitioner*, 13.

32. Walker, *Designing Sustainability*, 91.

Resources

Creative sector codes of ethics

GENERAL CREATIVE INDUSTRIES

The Canadian Creative Industries | Code of Conduct to Prevent and
Respond to Harassment, Discrimination, Bullying and Violence
readthecode.ca

ADVERTISING AND MARKETING

American Advertising Federation | Institute for Advertising Ethics
aaf.org/AAFMemberR/Efforts/AAF_Ethics/Institute_for_Advertising_
Ethics.aspx

The Canadian Code of Advertising Standards
adstandards.ca/code/

Canadian Marketing Association | CMA Code of Ethics and Standards
of Practice
the-cma.org/regulatory/code-of-ethics

ARCHITECTURE

The American Institute of Architects | 2018 Code of Ethics and
Professional Conduct
aianova.org/pdf/codeofethics.pdf

Architectural Institute of British Columbia | Code of Ethics and
Professional Conduct
aibc.ca/about/regulatory-authority/codes/

International Ethics Standard Coalition | The Standards
ies-coalition.org/standards/

Ontario Association of Architects | OAA Code of Ethics
oaa.on.ca/the+oaa/about+the+oaa/code+of+ethics

Royal Institute of British Architects | Code of Practice for
Chartered Practices
architecture.com/knowledge-and-resources/resources-landing-page/code-of-practice-for-chartered-practices

CRAFTS

Craft Retailers & Artists for Tomorrow | Code of Ethics
craftonline.org/pages/CODE_OF_ETHICS

International Decorative Artisans League | Code of Ethics
decorativeartisans.org/Code-of-Ethics

Saskatchewan Visual Arts and Craft Sector | Industry Standards/
Best Practices
bestpracticestandards.ca

DESIGN: PRODUCT, GRAPHIC, AND FASHION DESIGN

The Academy of Design Professionals | 2017 Code of Professional Conduct
designproacademy.org/code-of-professional-conduct.html

AGDA | Australian Graphic Design Association Code of Ethics
agda.com.au/about/code-of-ethics

Association of Sewing and Design Professionals (Global) | Code of Ethics
sewingprofessionals.com/code-of-ethics

Chartered Society of Designers | Code of Conduct
csd.org.uk/about/code-of-conduct

Graphic Designers of Canada | Code of Ethics
gdc.design/ethics/code

International Council of Design | Best Practices
ico-d.org/resources/best-practices

Registered Graphic Designers | RGD/GDC/SDGQ Code of Ethics
rgd.ca/ethics

FILM, TV, VIDEO, RADIO, AND PHOTOGRAPHY

Canadian Broadcasting Standards Council | Canadian Association of
Broadcasters' Code of Ethics (2002)
cbsc.ca/codes/cab-code-of-ethics

CBC/Radio-Canada | Journalistic Standards and Practices
cbc.radio-canada.ca/en/vision/governance/journalistic-standards-and-practices

Federal Communications Commission | The Public and Broadcasting
fcc.gov/media/radio/public-and-broadcasting

FILM London | The Code of Practice for Location Filming in London
filmlondon.org.uk/filming_in_london/code

Georgetown University | Ethical Filmmaking
library.georgetown.edu/gelardin/ethical-filmmaking

National Press Photographers Association | Code of Ethics
nppa.org/code-ethics

No Film School | Code of a Filmmaker
nofilmschool.com/principles-code-of-a-filmmaker

Ofcom Broadcasting | The Ofcom Broadcasting Code
ofcom.org.uk/tv-radio-and-on-demand/broadcast-codes/broadcast-code

Photographers Without Borders | PWB Code of Ethics
photographerswithoutborders.org/code-of-ethics

Professional Photographers of Canada | PPOC Code of Ethics
ppoc.ca/about/ethics.php

IT, SOFTWARE, AND COMPUTER SERVICES

Association for Computing Machinery | ACM Code of Ethics and
Professional Conduct
acm.org/code-of-ethics

British Computer Society | BCS Codes of Conduct and Practice
cs.uct.ac.za/mit_notes/ethics/htmls/cho4so4.html

Canada's Association of I.T. Professionals | Code of Ethics
cips.ca/ethics

Harvard University Information Technology | IT Professional Code of
Conduct to Protect Electronic Information
huit.harvard.edu/it-professional-code-conduct-protect-electronic-information

IEEE Computer Society | Code of Ethics
computer.org/education/code-of-ethics

International Game Developer Association | Core Values & Code of Ethics
igda.org/about-us/core-values-and-code-of-ethics/

Accountable Journalism | Codes of Ethics: North America
accountablejournalism.org/ethics-codes/north_america

The Canadian Association of Journalists | Ethics Guidelines
caj.ca/content.php?page=ethics-guidelines

COPE | Guidelines
publicationethics.org/guidance/Guidelines

Elsevier | Publishing Ethics
elsevier.com/about/policies/publishing-ethics

International Federation of Journalists | IFJ Global Charter of Ethics
for Journalists
ifj.org/who/rules-and-policy/global-charter-of-ethics-for-journalists.html

J-Source | Codes of Ethics
j-source.ca/article/codes-of-ethics/

Wiley | Best Practice Guidelines on Publishing Ethics
authorservices.wiley.com/asset/Best-Practice-Guidelines-on-Publishing-
Ethics-2ed.pdf

MUSEUMS, GALLERIES, AND LIBRARIES

American Alliance of Museums | Code of Ethics
aam-us.org/programs/resource-library/governance-and-support-
organizations-resources/code-of-ethics/

American Library Association | Professional Ethics
ala.org/tools/ethics

Canadian Federation of Library Associations | CFLA-FCAB Code of Ethics
cfla-fcab.ca/wp-content/uploads/2019/06/Code-of-ethics.pdf

Canadian Museums Association | Ethics Guidelines
museums.ca/uploaded/web/docs/ethicsguidelines.pdf

International Council of Museums | ICOM Code of Ethics for Museums
icom.museum/wp-content/uploads/2018/07/ICOM-code-En-web.pdf

International Federation of Library Associations and Institutions |
IFLA Code of Ethics for Librarians and Other Information Workers
ifla.org/publications/node/11092

Library and Archives Canada | Code of Conduct: Values and Ethics
bac-lac.gc.ca/eng/about-us/Pages/code-conduct-value-ethics.aspx

The Library and Information Association | CILIP's Ethical Framework
cilip.org.uk/page/ethics

Museums Association | Code of Ethics for Museums
wmuseumsassociation.org/ethics

National Association for the Visual Arts | Code of Ethics for Publicly
Funded Galleries
visualarts.net.au/code-of-practice/26-code-ethics-publicly-funded-
galleries/

National Gallery of Canada | Code of Conduct
gallery.ca/sites/default/files/documents/policies/NGC_code_of_conduct_
en.pdf

Ontario Association of Art Galleries | Code of Ethical and
Professional Conduct
oaag.org/policies.html#ethicalconduct

MUSIC, PERFORMING ARTS, AND VISUAL ARTS

College Art Association | Standards & Guidelines
collegeart.org/standards-and-guidelines/guidelines/practices

Incorporated Society of Musicians | ISM Members' Code of Conduct
ism.org/advice/ism-members-code-of-conduct

The Indigenous Art Code | The Code
indigenousartcode.org/the-indigenous-art-code/

Not in Our House | Chicago Theatre Standards
notinourhouse.org/wp-content/uploads/Chicago-Theatre-
Standards-12-11-17.pdf

Respectful Workplaces in the Arts | Canadian Code of Conduct for the
Performing Arts
respectfulartsworkplaces.ca/code-of-conduct

We Have Voice | Code of Conduct
wehavevoice.org

Books for the Conscious Creative

AIGA. 2008. *AIGA Professional Practices in Graphic Design*. Edited by Tad Crawford. New York: Allworth Press.

Artists Guild Graphic. 2018. *The Graphic Artist's Guild Handbook: Pricing & Ethical Guidelines, 15th Ed.* Avon, MA: Adams Media.

Bannon, Fiona. 2018. *Considering Ethics in Dance, Theatre and Performance*. New York: Palgrave Macmillan.

Beauvoir, Simone de. 1948. *The Ethics of Ambiguity*. New York: Kensington Publishing Corp.

Bellacasa, Maria Puig de la. 2017. *Matters of Care: Speculative Ethics in More Than Human Worlds*. Minneapolis, MN: University of Minnesota Press.

Berman, David. 2009. *Do Good Design: How Design Can Change Our World*. Berkeley, CA: New Riders.

Beshty, Walead. 2015. *Ethics*. Cambridge, MA: The MIT Press.

Borrows, John. 2019. *Law's Indigenous Ethics*. Toronto, ON: University of Toronto Press.

Bouwer, Johan. 2019. *Ethical Dilemmas in the Creative, Cultural and Service Industries*. Milton Park, U.K.: Routledge.

Bowles, Cennydd. 2018. *Future Ethics*. East Sussex, U.K.: NowNext Press.

Chick, Anne and Paul Micklethwaite. 2011. *Design for Sustainable Change: How Design and Designers Can Drive the Sustainability Agenda*. Lausanne: AVA Publishing.

Collier, Paul. 2018. *The Future of Capitalism: Facing the New Anxieties*. New York: HarperCollins Publishers.

Cools, Guy and Pascal Gielen. 2014. *The Ethics of Art: Ecological Turns in the Performing Arts*. Amsterdam, Netherlands: Valiz.

Davisson, Amber and Paul Booth. 2016. *Controversies in Digital Ethics*. New York: Bloomsbury.

Elliot, David, Marissa Silverman, and Wayne Bowman. 2016. *Artistic Citizenship: Artistry, Social Responsibility, and Ethical Praxis*. New York: Oxford University Press.

Fawkes, Johanna. 2014. *Public Relations Ethics and Professionalism: The Shadow of Excellence*. Milton Park, U.K.: Routledge.

Felton, Emma, Oksana Zelenko, and Suzi Vaughan, eds. 2012. *Design and Ethics: Reflections on Practice*. Milton Park, U.K.: Routledge.

Fisher, Thomas. 2010. *Ethics for Architects: 50 Dilemmas of Professional Practice*. New York: Princeton Architectural Press.

Fry, Hannah. 2018. *Hello World: Being Human in the Age of Algorithms*. New York: W. W. Norton.

Fry, Tony. 2009. *Design Futuring: Sustainability, Ethics and New Practice*. Oxford: Berg.

Fry, Tony, Clive Dilnot, and Susan Stewart. 2015. *Design and the Question of History*. New York: Bloomsbury Academic.

Fuad-Luke, Alastair. 2009. *Design Activism: Beautiful Strangeness for a Sustainable World*. New York: Earthscan.

Glaser, Milton, Mirko Ilic, and Steven Heller. 2017. *The Design of Dissent, Expanded Edition: Greed, Nationalism, Alternative Facts, and the Resistance*. Beverly, MA: Rockport Publishers.

Harries, Karsten. 2008. *The Ethical Function of Architecture*. Cambridge, MA: The MIT Press.

Helfand, Jessica. 2016. *Design: The Invention of Desire*. New Haven, CT: Yale University Press.

Heller, Steven and Véronique Vienne, eds. 2003. *Citizen Designer: Perspectives on Design Responsibility*. New York: Allworth Press.

IDEO and Jane Fulton Suri. 2016. *The Little Book of Design Research Ethics*. Palo Alto, CA: IDEO.

Izzo, John and Jeff Vanderwielen. 2018. *The Purpose Revolution: How Leaders Create Engagement and Competitive Advantage in an Age of Social Good*. Oakland, CA: Berrett-Koehler Publishers.

Jedlička, Wendy. 2010. *Sustainable Graphic Design: Tools, Systems, and Strategies for Innovative Print Design*. New Jersey: John Wiley & Sons.

Kalbag, Laura. 2017. *Accessibility for Everyone*. New York: A Book Apart.

Kane, Eileen. 2010. *Ethics: A Graphic Designer's Field Guide*. Avon, MA: Adams Media Corporation.

Kara, Helen. 2018. *Research ethics in the real world: Euro-Western and Indigenous Perspectives.* Bristol, U.K.: Policy Press.

Klein, Naomi. 2019. *On Fire: The (Burning) Case for a Green New Deal.* New York: Simon & Schuster.

Klein, Naomi. 2014. *This Changes Everything: Capitalism vs. the Climate.* Toronto, ON: Knopf Canada.

Macneill, Paul, ed. 2014. *Ethics and the Arts.* Heidelburg, Germany: Springer Verlag GmbH.

Manuel, Arthur and Grand Chief Ronald Derrickson. 2017. *The Reconciliation Manifesto: Recovering the Land, Rebuilding the Economy.* Toronto, ON: James Lorimer & Co.

Manzini, Ezio. 2015. *Design, When Everybody Designs: An Introduction to Design for Social Innovation.* Translated by Rachel Coad. Cambridge, MA: The MIT Press.

Monteiro, Mike. 2019. *Ruined by Design: How Designers Destroyed the World, and What We Can Do to Fix It.* San Francisco, CA: self-published.

Moran, Seana, David Cropley, and James C. Kaufman, eds. 2014. *The Ethics of Creativity.* New York: Palgrave Macmillan.

Nichols, Bill. 2016. *Speaking Truths with Film: Evidence, Ethics, Politics in Documentary.* Berkeley, CA: University of California Press.

Papanek, Victor. 1984. *Design for the real world.* Chicago, IL: Academy Chicago Publishers.

Postman, Neil. 2005. *Amusing Ourselves to Death: Public Discourse in the Age of Show Business.* New York: Penguin.

Reilly, Maura and Lucy Lippard. 2018. *Curatorial Activism: Towards an Ethics of Curating.* New York: Thames & Hudson.

Resnick, Elizabeth. 2016. *Developing Citizen Designers.* New York: Bloomsbury Academic.

Roberts, Lucienne. 2006. *Good: An Introduction to Ethics in Graphic Design.* Lausanne, Switzerland: AVA Publishing.

Scalin, Noah and Michelle Taute. 2012. *The Design Activist's Handbook: How to Change the World (Or at Least Your Part of It) with Socially Conscious Design.* Blue Ash, OH: HOW Books.

Shaughnessy, Adrian. 2010. *How to Be a Graphic Designer without Losing Your Soul*. New York: Princeton Architectural Press.

Shea, Andrew. 2012. *Designing for Social Change*. New York: Princeton Architectural Press.

Simmons, Christopher. 2011. *Just Design: Socially Conscious Design for Critical Causes*. Avon, MA: Adams Media.

Singer, Peter. 2019. *Ethics into Action: Learning from a Tube of Toothpaste*. London: Rowman & Littlefield.

Sinnerbrink, Robert. 2015. *Cinematic Ethics: Exploring Ethical Experience through Film*. Milton Park, U.K.: Routledge.

Strickler, Yancey. 2019. *This Could Be Our Future: A Manifesto for a More Generous World*. New York: Viking.

Thunberg, Greta. 2019. *No One Is Too Small to Make a Difference*. New York: Penguin Random House.

Walker, Stuart. 2017. *Design for Life: Creating Meaning in a Distracted World*. Milton Park, U.K.: Routledge.

Walker, Stuart. 2014. *Designing Sustainability: Making Radical Changes in a Material World*. Milton Park, U.K.: Routledge.

Younging, Gregory. 2018. *Elements of Indigenous Style: A Guide for Writing By and About Indigenous Peoples*. Edmonton, AB: Brush Education.

Yunus, Muhammad. 2017. *A World of Three Zeros: The New Economics of Zero Poverty, Zero Unemployment, and Zero Net Carbon Emissions*. New York: PublicAffairs.

Ethics in industry

The 3% Movement
3percentmovement.com

The A11y Project
a11yproject.com

AIGA | Design for Good
aiga.org/design-for-good

Anxiety Tech
anxietytech.com

Architexx
architexx.org

The Association for Women in Architecture + Design
awaplusd.org

Building Equality in Architecture
beatoronto.com (Toronto)
beaatlantic.com (Atlantic)

Cannes Lions Awards
canneslions.com/awards/good

Canopy Planet
canopyplanet.org/tools/

Center for Humane Technology
humanetech.com

Decolonising Design
decolonisingdesign.com/statements/2016/editorial

Decolonization and Indigenization: A Guide for Frontline Staff, Student Services, and Advisors
opentextbc.ca/indigenizationfrontlineworkers/chapter/decolonization-and-indigenization

Decolonizing Practices
decolonizingpractices.org

Depatriarchise Design
depatriarchisedesign.com

Design Justice Network
designjusticenetwork.org

Design Justice Summit
colloqate.org/design-justice-summit

Diversity Arts Australia
diversityarts.org.au

Equity
equity.org.uk

GDC | Accessibility Design
gdc.design/accessibility-design

Global Award for Sustainable Architecture
citedelarchitecture.fr/en/event/global-award-sustainable-architecture-2019

John Maeda | Design in Tech Report
designintech.report

LafargeHolcim | Awards for Sustainable Construction
lafargeholcim-foundation.org/awards/6th-cycle

Let's Make the Industry 50/50 Initiative
5050initiative.org

Open Technology Institute
newamerica.org/oti

RGD | AccessAbility 2: A Practical Handbook on Accessible Graphic Design
rgd.ca/resources/accessibility/access

RGD So(cial) Good Design Awards
rgd.ca/programs/sogood-awards

Stage Sight
stagesight.org

Tech for Social Justice / #MoreThanCode
t4sj.co
morethancode.cc

TIME'S UP Advertising
timesupadvertising.com

Accessibility

Accessibility by Design
wcag2.com

Accessibility Design
gdc.design/accessibility-design

The ADA Checklist: Website Compliance Guidelines for 2019 in Plain English
medium.com/@krisrivenburgh/the-ada-checklist-website-compliance-guidelines-for-2019-in-plain-english-123c1d58fad9

Creative Users Projects
creativeusers.net/accessing-the-arts/

GitHub Accessibility Resources
github.com/ediblecode/accessibility-resources

Paralyzed Veterans of America
pva.org/research-resources/accessible-design/accessibility-resources/

A Place for All: A Guide to Creating an Inclusive Workspace
chrc-ccdp.gc.ca/eng/content/place-all-guide-creating-inclusive-workplace

W3C Accessibility Resources
w3.org/standards/webdesign/accessibility

W3C Web Accessibility Laws & Policies
w3.org/WAI/policies/

Decoloniality and social justice

Aboriginal Gathering Place Resources
aboriginal.ecuad.ca/resources/

Guide to Indigenous Land and Territorial Acknowledgements for Cultural Institutions
landacknowledgements.org

Indigenous Reconciliation Group
reconciliationgroup.ca

Reconciliation Canada
reconciliationcanada.ca/about/history-and-background/background

"Ryan McMahon's 12-Step Guide to Decolonizing Canada"
cbc.ca/radio/day6/ryan-mcmahon-s-12-step-guide-to-decolonizing-canada-1.4719567

Glossary

A

ableism
Discrimination in favour of able-bodied people.

accessibility
The quality of being easily reached, entered, or used by people who have a disability.

accountable capitalism
An act proposed by Elizabeth Warren derived from B (Benefit) Corporations whereby corporations take on the social responsibility of personhood and distribute wealth beyond shareholders.

activist
A person who campaigns to bring about political or social change.

analogue
Not involving or relating to the use of computer technology, as a contrast to its digital counterpart.

Anglocentric
A worldview centred on or considered from an English or Anglo-American perspective.

appropriation
The action of taking something for one's own use, without the owner's permission.

archetype
A very typical example of a certain person or thing. A prototypical model of beliefs and behaviours that others may emulate.

attention economy
Attention economics is an approach to the management of information that treats human attention as a scarce commodity. Particularly relevant in the internet age.

B

B Corporation
Certified businesses that meet the highest standards of verified social and environmental performance, public transparency, and legal accountability to balance profit and purpose.

bias
Prejudice in favour of or against one thing, person, or group unfairly compared with another.

C

capitalism
An economic and political system in which a country's trade and industry are controlled by private owners for profit, rather than by the state.

carbon offset
A reduction in emissions of carbon dioxide or greenhouse gases made in order to compensate for or to offset an emission made elsewhere.

circular economy
A circular economy is an economic system designed to eliminate waste and pollution through the continual use of resources.

clickbait
Hyperbolic or misleading online content whose main purpose is to attract attention and encourage visitors to click on a link to a particular web page.

co-creation/co-design
An innovation process in which participants (putative, potential, or future) are invited to co-operate with designers, researchers, and developers.

colonialism
The practice of acquiring full or partial political control over a nation or people, occupying and exploiting it economically, socially, and politically.

consumerism
The preoccupation of society with the acquisition of consumer goods.

co-operative
A business or organization that is owned and run jointly by its members, who share the profits or benefits.

copyright

Exclusive and assignable legal right, given to the originator for a fixed number of years, to print, publish, perform, film, or record literary, artistic, designed, or musical material.

corporate social responsibility (CSR)

A business model that supports a company being socially responsible to itself, its stakeholders, and the public.

Creative Commons

One of several public copyright licenses that enable the free distribution of an otherwise copyrighted work.

crowdsourcing

The practice of obtaining information or input into a project by enlisting the services of a large number of people, either paid or unpaid, typically via the internet.

D

dark patterns

A user interface design that intentionally tricks users into carrying out a task they might otherwise not do. Examples can include unknowingly signing up for recurring payments or including expensive add-ons with a purchase.

decoloniality

A method for restoration, reparation, and the ongoing social dismantling and critique of things like racism and sexism that resulted from colonization and Eurocentrism, untangling the production of knowledge from a primarily Eurocentric episteme. It is a critique of what is seen as the perceived universality of Western knowledge and the superiority of Western culture.

decolonization

The process of a state withdrawing from a colony, leaving it independent. Formerly considered a formalized process of handing over government control, it is now recognized as a long-term process involving bureaucratic, cultural, linguistic, and psychological divesting of colonial power.

democratize

Make (something) accessible to everyone.

depatriarchisation

See patriarchy

dissent

The expression or holding of opinions at variance with those previously, commonly, or officially held. Often in the context of activism.

E

echo chamber

A situation where ideas or beliefs are reinforced through the repetition of a closed system that does not allow for the free movement of alternative or competing ideas or concepts.

eco-efficiency

The state of goods and services when they satisfy human needs and improve quality of life while progressively reducing resource intensity and mitigating negative ecological impact.

ecosystem

A biological community of interacting organisms and their physical environment; also a complex network or interconnected system.

elitism

The advocacy or existence of an elite (a group considered superior in terms of ability or qualities to the rest of a group or society) as a dominating element in a system or society. The attitude or behaviour of a person or group who regard themselves as belonging to an elite.

equity

The quality of being fair and impartial. Supporting based on individual need rather than treating everyone identically.

ethics

Moral principles that govern a person's behaviour or action.

Eurocentric

Focusing on European culture or history to the exclusion of a wider view of the world; implicitly regarding European culture as preeminent.

F

fair trade
The practice of directly benefitting producers in the so-called developing world by buying straight from them at a guaranteed price.

fake news
Refers to fabricated news. Found in traditional news, on social media, or on fake news websites, this content has no basis in fact but is presented as being true and accurate.

First Things First manifesto
Reacting against an affluent Britain of the 1960s, this famous manifesto rallied against consumerist culture and tried to re-radicalize a design industry that the signatories felt had become lazy, uncritical, and dedicated to working for the advertising industry.

font licensing
End User License Agreement (EULA) that defines what usage of a font is legally allowed. It is important to read the EULA and understand its restrictions. For example, some licenses may allow a font to be used on a single computer, some may stipulate that the font is for web use only, and some may allow any use in perpetuity.

G

gender equity
Provision of fairness and justice in the distribution of benefits and responsibilities between women, nonbinary identities, and men.

genetically modified organism (GMO)
Any organism whose genetic material has been altered using genetic engineering techniques. There is debate about the long-term effects to human bodies and the planet from the creation and consumption of GMOs.

grants
A sum of money given by an organization, especially a government, for a particular purpose.

green hosting
Web hosts that actively work to carry out eco-friendly initiatives that mitigate the impact on the environment of the high-energy use and carbon dioxide (CO_2) output of the data centres they use. Hosts typically mitigate their impact through the use of renewable energy or carbon offsets.

greenhouse gases

Any of various gaseous compounds that absorb infrared radiation, trap heat in the atmosphere, and contribute to the greenhouse effect. The main greenhouse gases in our atmosphere are carbon dioxide, methane, nitrous oxide, and ozone. Scientific evidence indicates that these gases have potentially dangerous impacts to water levels and earth temperatures.

greenwashing

Intentional disinformation disseminated by an organization so as to present an environmentally responsible public image.

H

heteropatriarchy

The combination of male (patriarchal) and heterosexual dominance essentially describing the sex and gender bias prevalent among the elite ruling classes of nation-states.

Hippocratic Oath

The ethical oath taken by medical professionals to "do no harm."

homophobia

Irrational fear of, aversion to, or discrimination against homosexuals/homosexuality.

human-centred design

A design and management framework that develops solutions to problems by involving the human perspective in all steps of the problem-solving process.

I

inclusive design

Design that is usable by and accessible to the maximum number of people without the need for special adaptation or specialization. Design which includes as diverse a team of stakeholders as possible.

income inequality

The difference found in various measures of economic well-being among individuals in a group, groups in a population, or countries. Economic inequality sometimes refers to income inequality, wealth inequality, or the wealth gap.

Indigenous Peoples
> In Canada, a collective noun for First Nations, Inuit, and Métis peoples. The original settlers of a given region, in contrast to groups that have settled in, occupied, or colonized the area more recently.

L

LGBTQ2IA+
> Also described as the queer community. An evolving acronym, LGBTQ2IA+ includes lesbian, gay, bisexual, transgender, queer, questioning, two-spirit, intersex, and asexual people. The + aims to include the identities which language does not yet support or that fall outside of cisgender and heterosexual paradigms.

M

media tourism
> The act of breaking out of one's echo chamber (an environment, typically online, in which a person encounters only beliefs or opinions that coincide with their own) to experience opinions and ideas that differ from those in one's close circle.

misogyny
> A hatred of or discrimination against women.

morality
> Principles concerning the distinction between right and wrong or good and bad behaviour, or the extent to which an action is right or wrong.

moral philosophy
> The area of philosophy concerned with theories of ethics and the study of human conduct and values.

multidisciplinarity
> Combining or involving several academic disciplines or professional specializations in an approach to a topic or problem.

N

natural capital
> The planet's natural assets, including geology, soil, air, water, and all living things which make human life possible.

net neutrality

The principle that internet service providers treat all data on the internet equally, and not discriminate or charge differently by user, content, website, platform, application, type of attached equipment, or method of communication.

neuronormativity

Opposite of neurodivergence. Not displaying/characterized by autistic or other neurologically atypical patterns of thought or behaviour including mental illness. Having a brain that falls within the dominant societal standards of "normal."

non-governmental organization (NGO)

A non-profit organization that operates independently of any government. One whose purpose is to address social or political issues.

non-profit organization (NPO)

Organization dedicated to advancing social or environmental causes that uses the surplus of its revenues to achieve its purpose, rather than distributing income to the organization's leadership.

O

open-source

Denoting something for which the original source code, information, or file is made freely available and may be redistributed and modified.

othering

To view or treat a person or group of people as intrinsically different from and alien to oneself.

P

parachute design

Well-intentioned but paternalistic form of design intervention that "parachutes" in to high-need communities, especially in the so-called developing world, without the depth of understanding necessary to effectively contribute to resolving the problems faced by the people in those communities.

participatory democracy

Individual participation by citizens in political decisions and policies that affect their lives, especially directly rather than through elected representatives.

paternalism

The limiting of a person's or group's liberty or autonomy by an authority, intended to promote their own good. Paternalism can also imply that the behaviour is against or regardless of the will of a person and that the behaviour expresses an attitude of superiority.

patriarchy/depatriarchisation

A system of society in which men hold the power and women are largely excluded from it. The undoing of that system of society toward more equitable structures of power is depatriarchisation.

persona

A persona is a fictional character created to represent a user type that might use a site, brand, or product in a similar way.

personal information

The Personal Information Protection and Electronic Documents Act (PIPEDA) is a Canadian law relating to data privacy which governs how private sector organizations collect, use, and disclose personal information in the course of commercial business.

piracy

The unauthorized use or reproduction of another's work. The creators of fonts, films, and computer programs are often victims of piracy.

plagiarism

The nonconsensual use of someone else's intellectual property passed off as one's own.

planned obsolescence

A policy of producing consumer goods that rapidly become obsolete and so require replacing, achieved by frequent changes in design, termination of the supply of spare parts, and the use of non-durable materials.

post-truth

Relating to or denoting circumstances in which objective facts are less influential in shaping public opinion than appeals to emotion and personal belief; the 2016 Oxford Dictionaries Word of the Year.

prejudice
Prejudice, or bigotry, is an affective feeling toward a person or group member based solely on that person's group membership.

privilege
A special right, advantage, or immunity granted or available only to a particular person or group of people.

pro bono
Denoting work undertaken without charge, especially work for a client with a low income or a non-profiting entity.

proprietary eponym
A ubiquitous brand name or trademark that is used to refer to its generic class of objects. Kleenex is a common example.

protest
A statement or action expressing disapproval of or objection to something.

Q

quadruple bottom line
Aims to balance monetary profit with environmental, spiritual, and social benefit. The term was first coined and introduced into mainstream usage by Ayman Sawaf in a bid to factor in the return to one's spiritual self as an additional bottom line.

R

racism
Prejudice, discrimination, or antagonism directed against someone of a different race based on the belief that one's own race is superior.

reconciliation
The restoration of friendly relations. The government of Canada is working to advance reconciliation with Indigenous Peoples based on rights, respect, co-operation, and partnership.

reflexive consumption
The repeated use of a resource or product performed as a reflex, without conscious thought.

regenerative design
A process-oriented systems-theory-based approach to design. It describes processes that restore, renew, or revitalize their own sources of energy and materials, creating sustainable systems that integrate the needs of society with that of nature.

renewable energy
Energy from a source that is not depleted when used, such as wind or solar power.

Rights of Nature Movement
An ecocentric movement recognizing that nature (including trees, oceans, animals, etc.) has rights as humans have rights. It aims to balance what is good for human beings with what is good for other species and the planet as a whole, and recognizes that all life on earth is intertwined.

S

single-use
Made to be used once only. Often used to describe disposable plastic packaging in contrast to environmentally friendly products.

social enterprise
A social enterprise is an organization that applies commercial strategies to maximize improvements in financial, social, and environmental well-being. This may include maximizing social impact alongside profits for external shareholders.

social impact
The effect of an activity on the social fabric of the community and well-being of its individuals and families.

social innovation
The process of developing and deploying effective interventions to address systemic social and environmental issues in support of sustainable progress.

spec/speculative work
Any job for which the client expects to see creative work or a designed product before agreeing to pay a fee.

status quo
The existing state of affairs, especially regarding social or political issues.

stigmatization
If someone or something is stigmatized, they are unfairly regarded by many people as being bad or having something to be ashamed of.

sustainability
Meeting the present needs of human beings and nature without compromising the ability of future generations to meet their own needs. Considers sustainability of natural resources as well as social equity and economic development.

systemic problems
A systemic problem is due to issues inherent in the overall system, rather than due to a specific, individual, isolated factor.

T

transition town
Transition initiatives and transition models refer to the grassroot community projects that aim to increase self-sufficiency to reduce the potential effects of peak oil, climate destruction, and economic instability.

transphobia
Intense dislike of or prejudice against transsexual or transgender people.

triple bottom line
A triple bottom line broadens an organization's focus on financial return to include social and environmental considerations. It measures a company's social responsibility, economic value, and environmental impact. The term was coined in 1994 by John Elkington.

U

United Nations 2030 Agenda for Sustainable Development
The UN Sustainable Development Goals (SDGs) are a plan for peace and prosperity for people and the planet. They recognize the relationality between ending poverty and deprivations of other crucial needs like health care and education with addressing climate change and environmental preservation.

unique selling proposition (USP)
A marketing concept first proposed as a theory to explain a pattern in successful advertising campaigns of the early 1940s. Such campaigns made unique propositions to customers that convinced them to switch brands.

universal design

The design of products, services, and environments to enable accessibility and comprehension, and be used to the greatest extent possible by all people, regardless of age, size, or ability.

usability

Connected to the term *user experience*, it is the ease of access or ease of use of a digital product or service. The level of usability is determined by how readily a user may realize their intention in an experience.

V

virtue

Behaviour showing high moral standards.

virtue signalling

Publicly expressing opinions or sentiments intended to conspicuously demonstrate one's good character or the moral correctness of one's position on a particular issue.

W

wicked problems

Complex problems with solutions that are difficult or impossible to realize due to contradictory or changing requirements, such as climate change and public policy like health care and education. *Wicked* denotes a resistance to solutions and the complexity of interdependencies that make solutions extremely challenging without innovative approaches like design thinking.

Photo by Erika Lind

Kelly Small is an award-winning creative director, designer, and writer with deep roots in communication design, marketing, and advertising, and a special focus on ethical and inclusive practice. A proven creative leader, strategist, and affiliated design researcher with Emily Carr University, Kelly holds an interdisciplinary master's degree in design, with research focused on creative industry ethics, social innovation, and sustainability. Kelly lives in Toronto with their wife, Dahlia, and bonus kid, Evan.

This book has been consciously created, with maximal collaboration, sensitivity, research, and mindfulness of accessibility, clarity, and environmental impact.
— Kelly Small and the conscious creatives at Ambrosia